Scottish

Thoughts and

Reflections

Vol 5.

The fifth in a series since moving back to Scotland from South Africa in August 2018.

David R B Nicoll

Biography:

David was inducted as an International Poet of Merit with the International Society of Poetry in America in 1997 and made it to the semi-finals of a poetry competition there between 2000 selected poets from all over the world. He has had poetry published in South African and International magazines and newspapers and was listed in the International Who's Who of Poetry in 2012. He has released quite a number of poetry books, lots with matching photographs, also POKE POetic joKE books and Tattoo/Body Art books. He has also released CDs with poetry and music. All CDs to date recorded and produced in South Africa. Please check out his website with links to the books and CDs on www.davidnicoll.co.uk The CDs are also on YouTube!

Their have been lyric videos made from some select tracks which are also on the website as well as a performance videos by others section which is great performances by fellow Poets and Musicians in the days BC!

Before Corona!

Thanks to Stephan Seeber for the use of his photograph Chemtrails over the Alps!

As the cover for this book.

I would ask that no one take offence on any of the contents of this book, rather take it with a sense of humour!

Printed via Amazon.co.uk

First Printing, February 2021

ISBN 9798707604799

www.davidnicoll.co.uk

david@davidnicoll.co.uk

We care about the planet and all life forms on it, we also object to many planes leaving long white streaks all over our skies and blocking out our sunshine amongst other things. Please join us if you do as well.

Face book groups:

SMAAPP Scottish Musicians and Artistes Against the Poisoning of our Planet

And

Anti Geoengineering Scotland.

Previous publications:

All available on Amazon as Paperback or KDP versions.

Scottish Thoughts and Reflections Vol 1, 2, 3 and 4!

Thoughts and Reflections Vols 1, 2 and 3.

The Poetic Picture book Vols 1 and 2.

POKEs POetic joKEs

This is POKES 2,3 and 4!

South African Tattoos

Northern Hemisphere Body Art/Tattoos Vol 1

Northern Hemisphere Body Art/Tattoos Vol 2

All links on www.davidnicoll.co.uk

CDs all on YouTube:

David Nicoll and friends Vols 1,2 and 3

With great thanks to the many friends and musicians who contributed

To the making of these CDs through my years in South Africa.

In collaboration with

Great thanks to Mervyn Fuller and friends for his musical creations.

Created in Gaansbai, Cape Town, South Africa.

I was the lyricist in the band known as MAD,

Mervyn and Myself became freinds a number of years ago, he was a retired singer
Songwriter who used to play the music circuits in South Africa.

We lived a long way apart and every now and again he would phone me and say,

Write something about this! Then he would give me an idea which would spark me,

Would then write down the lyrics and send them to him. He would then decide

What type of song to make it, Rock, Reggae, Easy listening? Then put it together

And pull his friends Mike Pregnolatu to add lead Guitar and Mike Laatz on Saxophone.

The idea behind the MAD CDs is for you to listen to tracks

Where you resonate with the track titles.

Mervyn And Dave:

CDs

Treat it so!

This is MAD 2!

On Days like These!

The Best of MAD!

The Beat goes on!

On the Home Straight!

* = with matching photograph

\# = with matching illustration

Index:

Can!

Chemistry!*

Clock!

Come to!

Control you!*

Cosy retreat!*

Culling of Humanity!

Daddy!*

Democracy!

Despair!

Did say!

Do that now!

Down here!*

Energy!*

Ever ask why?*

Face!

Fiction!

Fly free!*

Forgiven!*

Freedom away!

Fuck you!*

Going away!

Goebells Doctrine!

Happening tomorrow!*

Happy New FEAR!

Humanity!

Heavens way!*

History!*

Head their way!*

If you do?*

Indians here!

Into you!*

Ionisation!*

Job!

Laboratory!*

Longer free!

Manifest!*

Mind Unfortunately!*

Morningmare!*

Musical Symphony!

Narrative blindly!*

New world to see!*

No Girls!

Of Humanity!*

On the flu!

One fifty!

Oot!

Other Yin!

Our History!*

Plans*

Previously!

Question to me!

React!*

Rest!

Rockefellers Lock Step 2010

Sacred Cow!*

Sale anyway!

Secretly!

Seedy!*

Silently!

Smokes as well!*

So true!

Spray!*

State capture!*

The Floor!*

The I Am Mantra!*

The Smokescreen!*

The TV!

Theorists In Conspiracy!

This is True!

Time!

To Drink!*

Too big!

Training History!

True!*

Valley!*

Viking Ancestry!

We Can See Through!

A Black Sheep?

Quite an

Amazing

Photo,

Portraying

Our

Time!

In the

Background,

Charles

Rennie

Macintosh!

A

Glasewegian,

Master

Designer

And

Architect,

Who,

Unmasked,

Looks

Sublime!

But

Now,

"He

Cannae

Breathe,

Richt,

Maest

O the

Time!"

I

See a

Black

Sheep,

Just like me,

Sitting

On the

Top

Of

An

Open

Bus,

Just being

Natural,

Normal

And

Free!

She really

Dosent need

The

Publicity,

In the days,

When things

Are

Just

Crazy!

With brother,

Grassing brother,

Dividing each other,

With,

Or

Against,

The

Authority!

Which is

Enslaving us,

In an

Open prison,

Run on

Rules and

Instructions,

By which,

You must abide!

Dont question them,

Just accept them,

They say,

That

They

Are on

Your side,

And doing it,

For your

Own good,

Then becoming

More

Like

Dictators?

Or

Possibly

Cult?

Where the

Publics,

Subjugation,

To them

Is

Paramount!

Already

The fines,

The

Financial

Penalty,

Freedom

Is gone

Now brother,

Cant

You see?

To bring you

To your kness,

Financially!

If you cant

Afford it,

Then

Grey walls,

You could

Log term,

Study?

The fine,

At

Sixty

Quid

Initially,

For doing

Something,

That did

No harm,

Had

No victim,

So why

A penalty?

Doubles

Each time,

That you

Are caught

After then,

Not so

Funny!

As attending

Lock Down

Protest meetings,

In another city!

To meet,

Speak

And

With

Common

Consent,

We

Cumulatively,

Non consent

To this

Forced

Imprisonment,

And

Rule making!

Over

Everything,

Business

And

Economy,

You are

Forsaking!

Telling us

That masks,

We must

Wear!

Got the

Programmed

Daily

Adience

In front

Of the TV,

Every day!

Who beleive,

Whatever,

To them,

That

You,

Say!

But,

Not

Everyone,

Feels

That

Way!

Isnt it

Strange,

Almost

Enough

To

Make

Me

Weep!

Have

A

Look

At the

Photo

And

See,

If,

You

Can

See?

A

Black Sheep!

A Happy New Year To All!

A

Happy New Year

To all

SMAAPP

Members

From the

SMAAPP team

We have had an

Interesting year!

And still

Beleive

That next year!

You

Should

Chase still,

Chase

Your dream!

We need

To get

The word out,

To more people,

And

God willing,

We will,

Be

Opening eyes

And

Wakening up,

The

Sleepers,

As

These

Times,

That we

Live

In,

Are

Extreme!

But,

With

Truth,

Light,

The

Creator

Of

The

Universe

And

Each other,

We will make,

A winning

Team!

Please

Continue

With

Your

Great posts,

Commentary,

Music videos

And

Every

Brilliant

Meme!

Happy

New Year

To all!

A way!

I saw the film

1984 last night!

It didnt look right!

Did not look good!

Everyone,

Under

Servitude!

Not allowed,

From your home,

To stray!

No being out

On the streets,

Alone

After dark,

In any way!

Seems like we,

Have now

Surpassed,

The

Film,

In many

A Way!

About CONTROL!!!

Weird eh?

We have

Had,

The

Flu,

In

Scotland'

Since

Time,

For us,

Began!

Actually,

Since the

Arrival,

Of

Man!

Why,

Is

It,

Such

A

Problem,

This year?

With people

Locked up,

In their

Own homes,

For a

Long time now,

Through the

MSM and TV!

Getting the

Daily

Controlling,

Programming

Dose of

Everchanging,

New laws,

Restrictions

And

Statistical

Fear!

Jobs,

Gone now,

Businesses,

Boarded!

While,

The

Billionaires,

Get

Richer,

Adding

To the,

Mountains,

Of

Wealth,

Already

Hoarded!

Told to

Wear masks

After people

Had stopped,

So much,

Dying!

Now,

All

Increasing,

Cases

Of,

Stress,

Anxiety,

Mental

I'll health,

Suicides,

Depression,

With many

Sighing!

Poverty,

Now being,

Their

Way,

Of

Life,

With

No

Denying!

Food banks

In great

Demand,

Its

Volunteers,

Surely,

Helping

And

Trying!

Because

Of the

Government's,

Reaction,

To this

Overhyped,

PLANNEDemic,

Leaving

Billions,

Of

People,

Globally

Crying!

"We

Need

A

Vaccine!"

The

Establishment,

Programmed

People,

And

MSM

Scream!

Bill (God) Gates

And

His

Vaccine

Company,

Owned

Mates!

Will

Make,

So

Much

Money,

That it

Is

OBSCENE!

Why?

Is the

Main subject

Globally,

This latest

SCAMMEDemic?

It is

Everywhere,

I know!

From

Europe,

South America,

Asia,

Australia,

New Zealand,

The

UK,

China

And

Borneo!

But,

It is,

Only

Listed,

As

The

24th,

Leading

Cause of

Death?

So,

What?

Is the

Big

Issue?

We would

Like to know?

Ramping up

The

Fear!

Going,

For

The

Soul!

The

Truth

Is

" It's

Not

About

A

Virus,

It's

About

CONTROL!!!

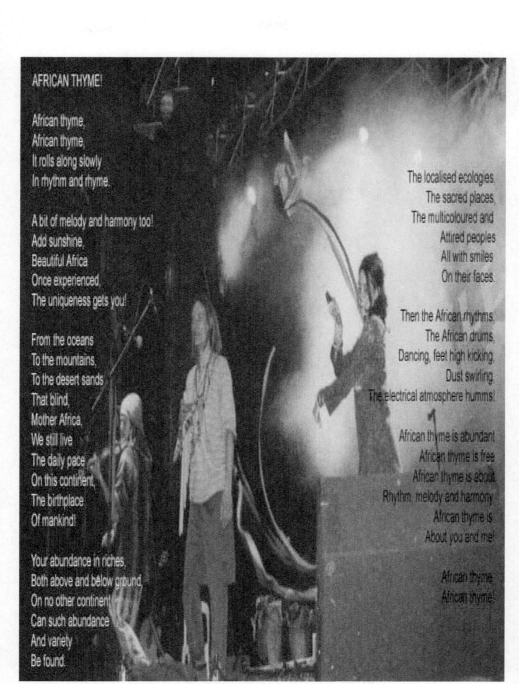

AFRICAN THYME!

African thyme,
African thyme,
It rolls along slowly
In rhythm and rhyme.

A bit of melody and harmony too!
Add sunshine,
Beautiful Africa
Once experienced,
The uniqueness gets you!

From the oceans
To the mountains,
To the desert sands
That blind,
Mother Africa,
We still live
The daily pace
On this continent,
The birthplace
Of mankind!

Your abundance in riches,
Both above and below ground,
On no other continent
Can such abundance
And variety
Be found.

The localised ecologies,
The sacred places,
The multicoloured and
Attired peoples
All with smiles
On their faces.

Then the African rhythms,
The African drums,
Dancing, feet high kicking,
Dust swirling,
The electrical atmosphere humms!

African thyme is abundant
African thyme is free
African thyme is about
Rhythm, melody and harmony
African thyme is
About you and me!

African thyme,
African thyme!

Alive Today!

There is

Banging,

Crashing

And

Fireworks

Flashing!

As it's

Guy Fawkes,

Day,

Today!

To signify

When he

Did try,

Many

Years

Ago,

To

Blow,

The

British

Parliament,

Away!

The

People,

Put

To

Task,

Will

No

Doubt,

Mainly,

Be

Wearing

A

Mask!

And

From

Others,

Staying

Two

Metres,

Away!

Because

Of,

New

Imposed

Laws!

They

Have,

Got

You,

By

The

Baws!

Not

Allowed

To

Go out,

In the

Evening,

To

Drink

And

Eat!

Not allowed,

To visit

Anyone,

Including,

Your

Granny,

To give

Her,

A

Wee

Treat!

Not allowed,

To visit,

Another

City,

Or

Town?

Not allowed,

To go out

For a beer,

Because,

All the

Pubs,

Have

Been

Forced,

To

Close,

Down!

Not allowed,

To see,

Your

Own

Family!

Because,

The

Country,

Is in

A

State,

Of

Lock Down!

Not allowed,

Too far,

From

Your

Home,

To

Stray!

Some,

Are

No doubt

Wishing,

That

Guy Fawkes,

Was

Still

Alive Today!

Already Know?

What a very

Strange virus,

We now

Have here!

Affecting the

Elderly!

With

Pre

Existing

Ilnesseses,

Mainly!

Also

The

Over

Eighty!

With

Written,

On almost

Every,

Death certificate,

Died

WITH,

Not

FROM,

C-V-D!

Here is

Bill

And

Nicola,

With

Smiles

On their

Faces!

The main

Fear

Nowadays,

Is all

To do,

With

Cases!

Cases,

Not being

People,

Who are

Unwell!

They

Just tested

Positive,

To a test,

But

Otherwise,

They feel

Well!

"Stay at home

For two weeks!"

The authorities,

Then tell!

If you dont,

It will wipe,

The smile,

From

Your face!

As they

Will fine you

One thousand

Pounds,

For going

Outside.

Noted by,

The new

System,

Of

Track

And

Trace!

All of us,

Now been

Locked down,

For

Three quarters

Of a year!

With a

Massive increase,

In

Suicides,

Drug addiction,

Alcoholism,

Depression

And

Anxiety,

All over

The place!

Daily breifings

On the TV!

For all

In the

Country,

To hear!

And

Worry!

No longer

Allowed

To see!

In any

Care homes.

Your father,

Mother,

Grandad,

Or

Granny?

Since last

March,

They have been

Living,

In

Solitary!

What a way,

To treat,

Our

Senior citizens,

Our

Elderly!

Unemployment

Skyrocketting,

With a

Deliberately,

Destroyed,

Economy!

With a

Great

Reset,

Now being

Proposed,

By

Klaus Schwab,

Head of the

World Economic Forum,

Prince Charles

And others,

In Authority!

Pushing for

A great

Reset!

With a digital

Passport,

Coming in,

Known as

ID 2020!

Also with

Bills involvement

Coincidentaly!

Now vaccines

Have suddenly

Appeared,

Not

Necissarily

Mandatory!

But it will,

Curtail

Yur freedom,

Ultimately!

If you remain,

Skin

Unpeirced

And

Unvaccinated,

Totally!

As to no

Concert

Or on

Public transport

Will you be

Allowed to go!

Or overseas travel

On aeroplanes,

To get away,

From the

Northern

Hemispheres,

Winter cold

And

Snow!

Putting

Pressure,

On you,

To go

With

The flow!

A

One

World

Government,

New

World

Order,

Is moving

In now!

Or,

Do that

Information,

You

Already

Know?

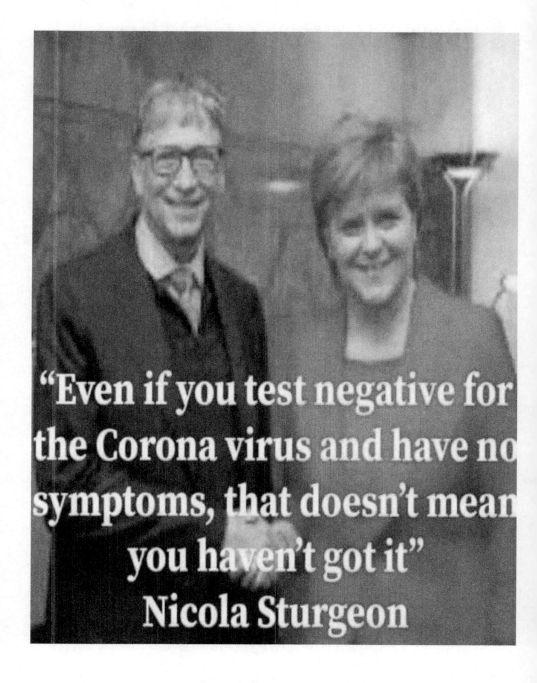

"Even if you test negative for the Corona virus and have no symptoms, that doesn't mean you haven't got it"
Nicola Sturgeon

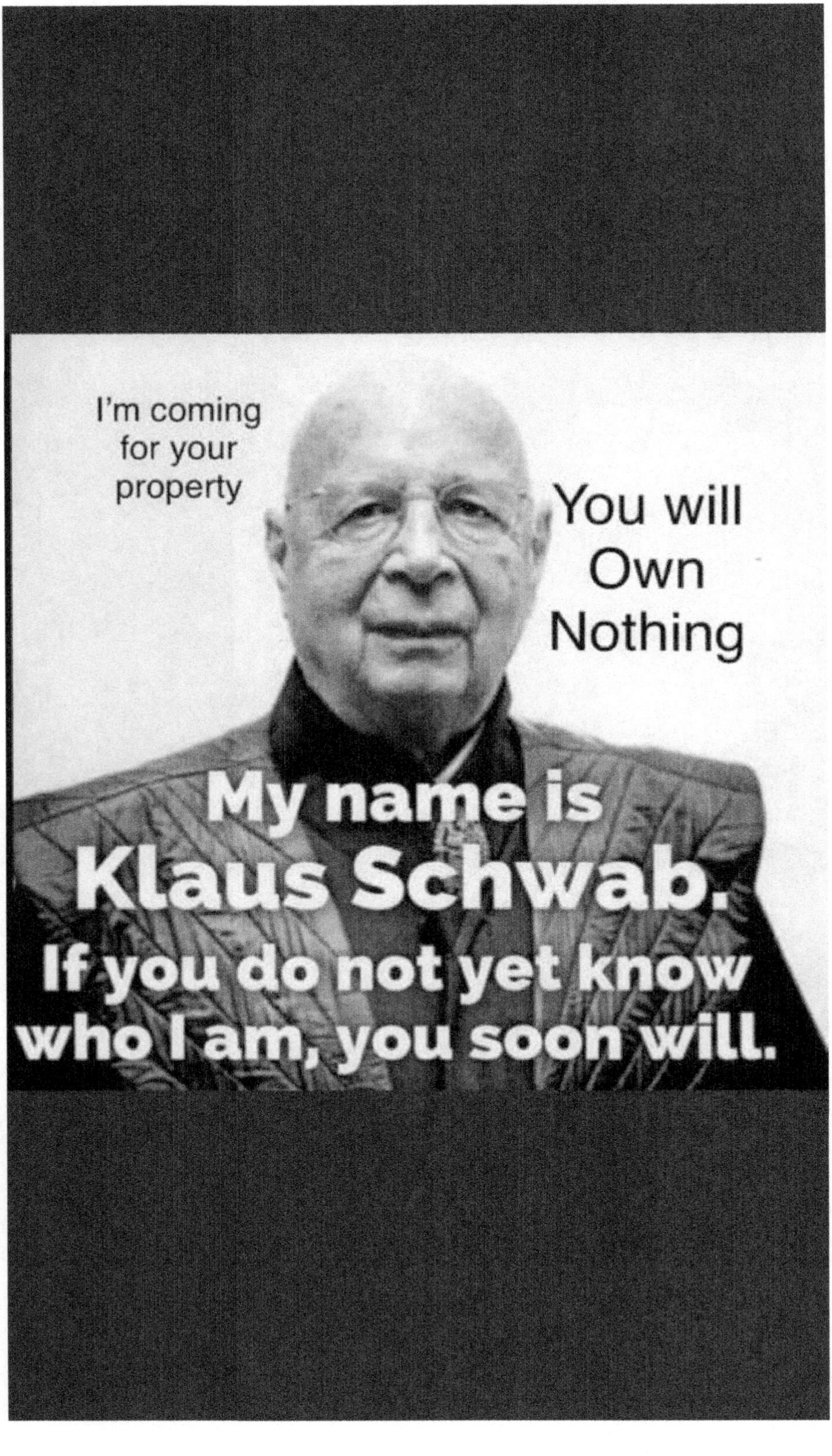
I'm coming for your property
You will Own Nothing
My name is Klaus Schwab.
If you do not yet know who I am, you soon will.

Andrew!

There were so many,

Pretty young mini skirted

Ladies in the Sea Angling club!

Honestly this is true!

Real candy for the eyes,

But now being a pensioner

I would have felt,

Like

Prince

Andrew!

Antique tractor!

Are Dead!

Can I tell

You a secret?

But you must not

Tell anyone!

The air that we breathe,

Is being poisoned,

It is really not fun!

Although this is

Only beleived by a few,

They try to tell the people,

Who dont beleive them!

Spreading the word,

Doing what they,

Can do!

Because ultimately,

These sprays,

Will affect

Everyone!

Look up

At the

Skies,

See it

In

Sun blocking,

Spreading lines,

With

Your own eyes!

Then dont tell

Your freinds

And family!

Because they

Will think,

That you are

Out of

Your head!

Better

Aware

And

Trying to

Change things,

Through

Awareness,

Before you,

Yourself,

Are

Dead!

Around here!

Crazy bloody

Situation,

That we

Find ourselves,

In today!

Leaves

The

Scots,

Not

In,

Good

Cheer!

We

Are

Not

Allowed,

To

Play,

Our

Bagpipes,

Even

Though

You are!

We

Also

Cant

Get

Any beer!

Something,

Is

Going on,

Around here!

Away!

There are over

Two thousand

Satellites,

In low

Earth orbit

Today!

That is going

To grow,

Exponentially,

If

Elon,

Has his way!

As he has

A contract,

To lauch

Forty thousand more,

In space

To stay!

Beaming

Down

60GHz mm

Microwaves,

Our way!

As well

As the

Chinese,

Indian

And

Russian,

Ones!

How many

Of them,

That their

Are going

To be?

Not sure

If

I

Could say?

But it is

Inevitable,

That

One day,

An

Asteriod,

Meteorite,

Or

Comet?

Will

Come

Heading

Our way!

And

Blow

One

Or

Two?

Of

Them,

Away!

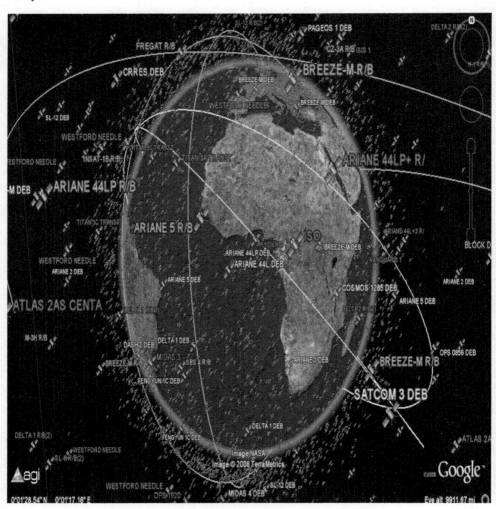

Bagpipes!

A question, does anyone have the answer to this?

Why is Scotland the only country in the WHOLE WORLD to ban the playing or

Practicing of the Bagpipes?

Replies:

Louise McIntyre

Because we're being run by a tyrannical government.

: cant argue with that.

Wull Boyle

Coz Sturgeons a Traitor !!!

: Cant argue with that either.

Dex Stewart

Because of the brainless Twatts who reside in the sheep shed called Hellyrude... That's why

Lewis Fowler

Because it's brings out the Scottish nationalism in us all, they can't do nothing just don't consent simple government and police can't do jack shit without consent

Andrew Smith

When did this happen? Never seen nowt about it. If that's true they can ram that law.

BC!

Do you

Want

To know,

The

Future?

Like

Gazing,

Into a

Crystal

Ball!

The

Following,

Steps,

Are

Showing

Plans,

Taken

From the

Rockefellers,

2010

Lock Step

Wall!

The future,

Then clearly,

You will see!

Knowing that

The

Governments

And

Corporations,

Will all act,

Accordingly!

To make,

These

Plans,

A

Reality!

From

October

2020,

Which is

Where

We are now!

Enact Phase 2

Quarantines!

Blame the

Protestors!

"Your

Freedoms

Have

Consequences"

Will be used,

Along with

Checkpoints!

No travel,

Replace fines,

With

Jail terms,

Deem all

Travel.

As

Non essential!

Not

Good scenes!

Increase,

Track

And

Trace,

Have

Facial,

Recognition

Cameras,

Installed,

All

Over,

The

Place!

Create

Food

Shortages,

Destroy,

The

Global,

Economy!

Make

Phase 2

Much

Longer,

To

Lower

Peoples,

Immunity!

Only

Essential

Goods,

Will

You

Be able

To

Buy!

Unless,

You are

First given,

Permission,

To do so,

By those,

On

High!

They will use

Extreme actions

Or

Force?

To quell

Any public

Outrage!

As indeed

Has

Happened

Already,

In

Trafalgar Square,

When many

Riot police,

Attacked

Peaceful,

Protestors,

Just

Behind,

The

Stage!

Batons

Out,

Smashing

Into

Innocent,

Skulls,

Acting,

As if,

In a

Rage?

Make

Anyone,

Who

Appears

To

Defy

Them,

As

Public

Enemy

Number

One!

Already that

Is happening,

To

Individual

Innocent citizens

And for them,

It is not

Fun!

The price

For

Speaking out,

Their

Truth!

Know

One thing,

Without a

Doubt!

The

Truth,

No matter,

How

You

Supress it,

Always

Finds,

A way,

To

Get out!

Six

Month

Long,

Second

Lock Down,

Roll out

The

Vaccines!

Make them

Mandatory!

With

Certification

And

ID 2020!

Food

Shortages,

Amplify!

Blame

The non

Vax takers,

As the

Cause

Of all

The

Problems!

People will

Fight against,

Each other

And

Cry!

"They are

Hurting our

Way of life!"

The

Vax

Partakers,

Will

Sigh!

Setting

People,

Against

People,

The

Age

Old

Tactic,

Of

Divide

And

Rule!

Victimise

The non

Vax takers!

As being

To others,

Health

Forsakers!

Limit

Their

Ability,

To

Work,

Travel,

Or

Live?

No

Help,

To

Them,

Will

You

Give!

If the

People

Are in

The

Majority?

That a

New

Vaccine,

They,

Do not

Want

To see!

Then,

There

Will

Be,

Released

A

More,

Virulent,

Virus,

Affecting

The

Population,

In

Percentage,

About

Thirty!

In

Phase

Three!

To make

The

Minority,

The

Majority!

Enact the

Start

Of a new

Economy!

In

Crypto

Currency!

Microsoft

Patent,

060606

Funnily!

Which is

Based,

On

Bodily,

Activity!

Fed

Data

From

The

Chip

Known as

The

RFID,

Which

Was in the

Vaccination,

If you take it?

And now,

Could be?

Inside your

Body!

An

Amazing

Thing now,

Technology!

With

60GHz mm

Microwaves,

Buzzing

Around,

Many a

Global city!

Going onto

A

Social

Credit,

System,

Where

You

Will be,

No longer,

Free!

They will

Then control,

Your

Destiny!

Removing

Access

For you,

To one

Or

Another?

Basic

Commodity!

If your

Credit score

Goes down,

You will

Have

Difficulty,

To survive

You see!

Welcome

To

The

New

World

Order!

Things

Were

Better,

In the

Days,

BC!*

*=Before

Corona!

Beer!

Students stuck

In dormatories,

All kept

In isolation,

Due to the

Latest viral

Dis-ease!

They

Were quite

Clever,

Although,

No doubt,

Living

Under fear!

They had

The foresight

To

Send

Out

A

Visual

SOS,

For

Some,

Beer!

Being free!

Just read the

Rockefellers,

Lock Step

2010

Document,

It

Is

All

There,

The

Future,

In

Black

And

White!

Looks like

Our future,

Is planned

Before us,

The way,

That

They,

Want it,

To be!

A

New

One

World

Government

Of

Tyranny!

Where

No one,

Will

Be

Free!

All

Part,

Of

The

IOT!

Being

Installed,

At this

Very moment,

Surrepticiously,

60 Ghz mm

Microwave,

Technology!

Under the

Smokescreen,

Called

C-V-D!

Creating a

Hyped up,

Orchestrated,

Sense of

Emergency!

Taking over all

The MSM

And on

Every TV!

Every day,

They see!

Statistics,

With

Inflated

Figures,

Creating,

Fear!

In those

Who see!

Using it to

Lock down,

Every business,

And workplace,

Destroying

The

Worldwide,

Economy!

Insisting on rules,

Mask wearing,

Social distancing,

No travelling,

No visiting!

No live music

Allowed,

Not allowed

To even sing!

Only twenty

People

Allowed

Now,

When

You

Exchange,

A

Ring!

Same,

When

You

They are

Burrying!

No travelling

To any

Other city!

In another area,

More is

The pity!

As we

Have

Lock Down

Protest

Meetings

At

Holyrood

Once a month

In

Edinburgh,

Another

City!

We

Are not,

Mask wearers

All

Free

From

C-V-D,

As we

Beleive,

That it

Is all,

Set up

For

Control!

In a

Projected

Fear,

With

Inflated figures,

That turned

Out,

Not quite

To be,

But gave

The

Government,

Who

Actually,

Work

"FOR

US!"

Powers

In

A declared

Pandemic,

Emergency!

That they

Would not

Normally have,

But received,

Them now

And are

Using them

With

Vigour

And

Alcracity!

Giving the

Politicians

The powers

To strip us

Of our

Human

Rights,

Imposing

Unemployment,

Despair,

Depression,

Suicides

And

Poverty!

Soon

Also

In

Scotland,

With the

New

Hate

Speech

Bill,

Speech,

Will no

Longer

Be

Free!

All it takes,

Is for someone,

To take offence,

To anything,

You said,

In the

Present?

Or even,

In your

History?

Where

You,

Could be?

Taken to

Court

And

Sued

Mercilessly!

By

A

Possibly,

Over

Zealous

Prosectutor,

With a

Tainted

History?

Tagged,

Named

And

Shamed!

Also

No doubt,

To keep

Attitudes

Inflamed!

More

Restricted

Every

Day,

By

A

One

World

Government,

Pushing its,

Globalist tactics,

Keeping the

Global population,

Under house arrest,

With changing rules,

Constantly,

No one knowing

What is

Coming.

Next?

I tell

You what,

These times

That we

Live in now,

Are

Definative!

We will

Always,

Remember

The

Year

Of

2020!

As

The

Year,

When

Mankind

Was

Stopped

From

Being free!

THE SEER
"You are not a poet,
You are in fact a bard,
And you are!"
What exactly did Helen mean?
A dictionary check
Would enlighten this scene,
A poet is one who likes to write in rhyme,
Or who has great imagination and creativity.
Most of the time.
A bard is
"One of an ancient order of Celtic Poets",
Also writers of rhyme but in built into your,
DNA and Heritage, most of the time.
A recollection to Washington,
At an international Poet's convention,
By a fellow Scots poet,
A man of wisdom and good cheer,
He referred to me not as,
David Nicoll,
But as "Macleod Of Macleod - "The Seer".

Before C-V-D!

Oh,

How

Great,

Life was,

In the

Days,

Of

BC!

Remember

Then,

Before,

Last

March,

When

We,

Were

Free!

To

Do,

As

We,

Wanted!

To

Follow,

Our

Own

Course

And

Destiny!

To

Travel,

Freely,

To

See,

To

Listen

To

Live music

In the pubs,

And

Poetry!

The

Theatres,

For some,

Or

Orchestral,

Symphony?

Now,

What,

Can

You do?

Honestly!

Do

You,

See?

How

All

The

New,

Imposed

Rules,

Regulations

And

Laws,

Are

Eroding

And

Diminishing,

Our

Human rights,

And

Taking away,

Our

Liberty!

Bit

By bit,

Slowly,

Slowly!

Could

This be?

A

Global

Conspiracy?

Where

One group,

Is going,

For

Global,

Supremacy?

To

Introduce,

Us ,

To

The,

IOT*

With

60GHz mm

Microwaves,

Metallic

Nano.

Particulates,

In

Overhead

Sprays!

That

Create,

So many,

Sun hidden,

Grey days!

Then

Of course,

You

Will need,

A couple

Of

Jags,

In

Bum?

Or

Arm?

Of

Untested

And

With

Potentially,

Problematic

Ingredients,

Which for

Some,

May

Cause

Alarm?

An

Added

Ingredient

Will be!

A

Chip

Known

As

An

RFID!

To take

Away,

Your

Individuallity!

Word has it,

That also,

Of your

Parenting

Ablities,

As far as

Procreation,

Goes,

They would,

Strip!

Not funny

Ingredients,

Check them

Out

And

You will see!

Formaldehyde,

Sterility

Agents,

Aluminuim,

And

Mercury!

Now,

These

Things,

In your

Body!

Should

Not be!

But is done,

In the rushed

Overexpressed

And hyped,

Emergency!

That

"The

Whole

Global,

Population,

Must be

Vaccinated,

You see!

Said

Bill (God) Gates

On the

TV!

And

The vaccine

Makers

With

Immunity,

For any

Potential,

Catastrophe!

That will

Happen

In some

Cases

Inevitably!

With

Everyone

Focused,

On a

Global

Fear,

Of

Dying

From

C-V-D!

Truth is,

No one,

Dies

From

it,

Only

With

it,

There

Is a,

Big

Difference,

Their!

But the

MSM

And

TV!

Constantly,

Keep

Regurgitating

Updating,

Keeping up,

The

Scare!

Tieing the

People down,

Where has gone,

Democracy?

The politicians,

Giving themselves,

Elevated powers,

Due to the

WHO,

(After

Receiving

50 Million

From Bill)

Declaring

A

Pandemic

Emergency!

Enabling them,

To enact

Rules and laws,

To restrict us,

And tie

Us down,

Potentially,

Endlessly?

Also

Giving them

The powers,

To fine us,

For

Breaking,

Any

Of these,

New laid,

Down

Conditions,

To our

Day to day,

Hum drum

And

Extremely

Limited

Routines,

But still,

They

Think,

That

We,

Should

Pay!

A lot

Of

Money,

To

Make

Profits

For the

Corporations

Including

Law and Order,

That exist

Today!

Go back

Twelve months!

What were

You doing?

Was

Everything,

OK?

Now,

Compare it,

With where

You are

Today!

Look,

How

Many

Freedoms,

Have been

Taken away!

What

Are you?

No

Longer

Allowed

To do!

There are

So many,

Do you

Honestly,

Beleive

That

This,

Is all

Because

Of

The flu?

They are

Conning me,

They are

Conning you!

Please,

Join your

Local

Lock Down

Protest group,

As in numbers,

That,

Is the

Only way,

Through,

With

Fellow

People,

Who can

See

Through!

The

Globally

Imposed

Insanity!

Ruining,

The

Whole

Global,

Ecomony!

March 23rd

2020!

That is

The day,

That

Marks,

The

Term

BC,

Before C-V-D!

Bill (God) Gates!

He is

Funding

The

Spraying,

Of

Toxic

Particles,

In the

Global air!

Leaving

Many,

With

Dementia,

Altzheimers

And

Many

Another,

Serious

Issue,

Needing

Medical care!

Geoengineering,

They call it,

To block,

Out

The Sun,

They

Spray,

Then the

Nexrads,

Dopplers

And

HAARPs,

Are

Turned on

Creating lines,

In the Spray!

Which then,

Spread out

And

Hide,

The

Sun,

Away!

All

Over

Grey!

Sometimes,

This can last,

For many

A day!

Stops your

Vegetables;

From

Growing so well,

Fruit trees

Reportedly,

Not doing

Very well!

Reduced

Sunlight

Is not good

For any

Life forms,

Not matter what

Anyone

Does say!

But he

Makes

Choices,

Over us,

On manys

A day!

Billionaires

Mainly,

Some

Are

Mates,

With

Our

New,

World

Leader,

Mr Bill (God) Gates!

and that was the day that Bill Gates decided to murder all of humanity

Boiling Frogs!

Wise words

There Dave,

It looks like,

There is nothing,

That we can

Do about it?

Or is there?

The New

World order

And

One

World

Government

Is on its way!

By locking us all up,

In our own homes,

With new,

Restrictive

And

Draconian laws,

Being brought out,

Each day!

Because,

Of a

Man made,

And

Patented virus,

Orchestrated,

All over the globe,

No one is allowed,

To go to work,

Socialise,

Venture too far,

From home,

Otherwise

Big fines,

Or jail terms,

Will be coming,

Your way!

Families stuck inside,

With nothing to eat!

A screaming wife

And three kids,

That all the

Time just greet!*

For some,

Life,

At the moment,

Is not,

At all sweet!

Virus statistics,

Being manipulated,

Most testing positive,

On the

Death certificate,

You will see!

Died,

(WITH)

COVID!

There are no more,

People dying now,

Than there were,

This time last year!

It's not like it is,

A killer pandemic,

This is a grab,

For the Soul,

And all,

The regulations,

About,

Self isolation,

Self imprisonment,

Social distancing,

One exercise,

Period a day!

A one hour walk,

Half an hour run,

Or three quarters,

Of an hour,

Cycling,

The new laws say!

It's all,

Just for control!

Step out of line,

Then you,

Will,

Get hit,

With a

Massive fine!

I believe that,

In South Africa,

You cannot,

Even buy,

Fags or wine?

What on earth,

Has that,

Got to do?

With,

Getting

Or giving?

Someone

The Flu?

You see people,

Out here

In Glasgow

Walking,

Their dogs!

My opinion is,

That the,

World's

Population,

Is,

Getting

Treated,

Like

Boiling

Frogs!

*= Crying

Thanks for the inspiration

David Marks.

Boy!

"You

Know,

You

Have

Raised,

A

Pervert,

Here!"

She

said

So

Coy!

I

Thought

To

Myself,

"Mmmm,

That's

Ma

Boy!"

Brother!

Ah

OK,

Mark,

How

Is life

With you?

And in

Knysna?

Scotland,

Is a

Fuck up,

All these

Bloody,

Rules

And

Regulations,

About

A

Flu!

We have

Had

Flu

Here

Since

Time began,

This one,

Is no worse,

Than

Any other!

What,

They

Are

Not

Telling us,

Is,

That

Like,

 George Orwell

Said,

These,

Are

Now,

The

Days,

Of

Big

Brother!

Can be!

Well here

We are,

Another

New Year,

But

Everyone

Is going

Into

This one,

Not

Exactly

Full of

Good cheer!

As

We,

Have been

Stopped

From

Meeting

Our

Freinds

And

Family,

Told

To

Stay

At

Home,

Unfortunately!

Just

Keep

On

Reading

The

Newspapers

And

Watching,

The

TV!

The

Vaccines,

Are

Here

Now,

So,

We

Will,

Give

You,

A

Jab

Or

Three?

We

Have

Taken

Away,

Your

Freedom

And

Liberty!

Do

You

Not

See?

Dear

Lord,

How

Gullible.

Some

People,

Can be!

Can!

Live!

Live!

While

You

Can!

Time,

Is

Precious,

Makaplan!

Do,

What,

You,

Can!

Chemistry!

It

Absolutely,

Astounds

Me,

That

These,

Long

White,

Spreading

Streaks,

In the sky,

Are

Invisible,

To

The

Majority!

Why do

They,

Not see?

This

Sun blocking,

Poisonous,

Cocktail,

Of

Chemistry!

Come to?

Got told

A story,

Still to

Vefify,

If it is true!

In

South America,

Baby foeteses,

Are for sale!

And it is,

A big,

Business,

Too!

They are

Used,

To make

Vaccines

And as

Satanic

Rituals!

What on

Earth,

Has the

World,

Come to?

Control you!

Strange days,

That we

Live in,

Today!

Where

Everyone,

Is

Supposed

To wear

A

Mask,

If from

Their home,

They

Stray!

It was

Not

Always,

That

Way!

But now,

It is

The norma1,

If you dont,

Wear one,

You

Stand out.

Like a

Black Sheep!

With a

99.0% chance

That it

Will not

Affect you,

And a

90 percent,

Recovery rate,

Tell me,

Why,

Are you,

So blue?

Please

Remember,

Whatever

You do!

That this

Whole hype,

Is only,

About

The flu,

The

TV!

Telling you!

Everything,

That you,

Must do!

Cutting

Down,

On your

Bodily

Intake,

Of

Oxygen,

Will not,

Be good,

For you!

This

Is

True!

Do you

Not see?

That

Fear,

Is

Used,

To

Control

You?

Cosy Retreat!

Its

January,

In

Scotland!

And

Things,

Are

Getting,

Cold!

Sometimes,

During

The day,

Into

My

Sleeping

Bag,

On

Top

Of

The

Bed,

Into

Its

Warmth,

I

Fold!

Looks

Like,

I

Am

Not,

The

Only

One,

That

Likes

Its

Heat!

Ginger,

The

Cat,

Has

Found,

A

New

Cosy,

Retreat!

Culling Of Humanity!

Trying to make

Sense of this,

It dosen't

Seem right

To me!

Having worked

Previously,

With some

Involvement of

Workers

Health and Safety!

Wearing masks

Full time,

Is not

For you,

Healthy!

As you

End up

Reinhaling,

Your exhaled

Carbon dioxide,

With bacterial

Build up,

Inside

The masks,

Will leave you,

With problems

On your

Face,

With issues,

Respiratory!

Or

Possibly?

Even,

Pluerisy?

It is

Only

A

Matter of time,

For each

Individual

You see!

The

Insane

Thing

Is that

it is

Becoming

Mandatory!

How on

Earth

Can

This

Be?

To

Encourage

And

Impose,

An

Unsafe

Act,

On

The

Majority!!!!!!!

To

Make

Them

Sick,

Ulimately!

Is

This

Agenda

2021

And

30?

A

Culling

Of

Humanity?

Daddy!

At this

Moment in time,

The future

For

Humanity,

Looks,

Bleak!

But lots

Dont know,

Or even

Think about

Things?

As

They,

Are

Conditioned,

By the TV

And

MSM

24/7

Every day,

Of

Every week!

All

The

Watchers

Minds,

Focused,

Hypnotised,

On the flu

And how,

It can

Kill you!

So sit

At home,

Dont talk,

To

Anyone!

Is what

They want,

You to do!

And if

You dont,

They will

Heavily fine,

Or

Arrest you?

Keeps the kids

At home,

Dont let them

Roam!

No dreams

Ahead,

Billions

Of

People,

Bored,

Out of

Their

Head!

Suicides,

Bankruptcies,

Poverty,

Anxiety

And

Depression,

Driving people,

Out of their

Head!

With the

Masses,

Getting

The

Latest

Doses,

Of

Statistical,

FEAR

Porn

And

Instructions

Through

The TV!

While above

Their heads,

Outside,

The skies

Get

Criss crossed

With toxic

White

Spreading sprays,

Geoengineering!

And its

Sun dimming ways!

Done in the open,

For all to see!

But done

At the

Same time,

Very

Quietly!

And

Discreetly!

No mention

Of it

Anywhere,

Actually!

Does the

Weatherman,

Or

Commercial pilots?

These things,

Never see?

All owned

And

Controlled

Unfortunately!

Bill (God)Gates,

Must be

Playing,

With his

Calculator

Now,

Working

Out the

Profit margins

On

7 Billion

Injections,

Each year,

Indefinitely!

On

Second thoughts,

Maybe,

You will be

Extremely

Lucky,

To

Actually

Make it

To

Three!

At a

20

To one,

Return,

On his

Investment

And

Less people

On the

Planet!

Happy

He

Would be!

And

No doubt,

If he was

Still Alive,

So would,

His

Eugenicist,

Daddy!

Democracy?

From Claire Davies:

"So looks like lockdown till July 17th ... so the two weeks to flatten the curve was obviously just teeing us up for getting used to the great reset and new world order agenda.

Masks are now normal, vaccines are accepted widely as the saviour. Even though they don't protect you from the virus or stop you spreading it.

Businesses are crushed. People are lonely and demoralised and we are so isolated that we will lose our ability to come together to challenge the oligarchy to change the path we are on. Even if we could organise anything we have lost our freedom and the right to protest.

It doesn't matter anyway because the psy-op has worked so well. Why wouldn't it? The elite nazis and best psychological profilers in the world are behind this. If you ask about the safety of a vaccine you're anti vax, Facebook doctor and shamed and vilified. If you don't wear a mask you are shunned and shamed for being selfish. Even though there's no scientific proof masks work. To be honest, common sense must tell us they don't because the infection rate has gone up since they have been mandatory!

What a glorious time to be alive! teenagers robbed of their fun years. Men demoralised losing incomes and feeling hopeless. Elderly dying in homes with no visitors or hugs or human warmth. No weddings, Christenings or family gatherings where we feel a sense of belonging and togetherness and all because the BBC and media (that's owned by five billionaires) chose to scare you so much that you've become so afraid of dying from a virus with a 99% plus recovery rate that you're not living.

At what point is enough enough? Or are we just being programmed to accept a police state new world order dictatorship that serves the ruling elite and dehumanises and demoralises the rest of us. Strange times indeed".

Couldn't have put it better.

☺🩶

David Nicoll

Extremely well said Claire Davies ! Remember this PLEASE Twelve months ago, we were FREE!!! Where now, is Democracy?

Despair!

I love these

Lightly sea salted,

Kettle fried crisps!

They are

Beyond compare!

The first thing

That

You notice is

That the bag'

Is full of,

Air!

As

Is

Common,

Nowadays!

To

Eveyones,

Despair!

Did Say!

There is a

Three man band

From

Stornoway!

Called

Peat and Diesel,

Who did a

Three lorry tour,

Through their

Hometown,

Last

Wednesday!

On the back,

Of the one

Covered truck,

They all

Did play!

With the

Trucks hooters,

Constantly

Blowing away!

To let

The locals know,

That something,

Was happening,

That dark

Rainy day!

Apologising

To

The

Police later,

"Easier

To

Apologise,

Than gain

Permission,

From them!"

They,

Did say!

Do that now!”

Isn't it

Amazing,

How

Things

Change!

What

Was once

No

Problem,

Is now,

A

Sacred

Cow!

“My

Parents

Used

To have

A

Pub,

Called

The Black Bitch!

But they

Couldn't

Possibly,

Do that now!”

Down here!

Where is

America headed?

As far as

Food production

Does go?

With

Bill Gates,

Being the number

One owner

Of

Farmland there!

Things will

No doubt,

Now move fast

And not slow!

As he is a

Big investor

In

Monsanto!

Whose crops

Are mainly,

GMO!

With

Round up

And

Glysophate,

Sealing manys

Fate!

As we,

Already know!

Now

President Biden

Has just appointed

Tom Vilsack,

To head the

USDA!

Which for

Humanitarians,

Conservationists

And

Ecologists,

Will come as a

Blow!

As his nickname

Is

Mr Monsanto!

All,

No doubt,

Part of the

Corporations plans,

Although,

We did

Not know!

The whole world

Is being

Hijacked,

At the moment,

In case,

You did

Not know!

Holding

The worldwide,

Population,

In a state

Of

FEAR!

Look at

How much,

Things

Have changed,

Just within,

The last

Year!

Who now,

Is in

Good

Cheer?

Apart

From the

Billionaires,

Who towards,

Darkess

And

Satanic

Influence,

Humanity,

They steer!

Dear God,

Creator

Of the

Universe!

Right now,

We need

Your help,

Down here!

Energy!

Young

Brothers

In

Arms,

Experiencing

Natures

Charms!

A

Bright

Future,

Do

They,

Forsee?

As

They,

Check

Out,

The

Power,

Of

Natures

Energy!

Ever ask Why?

<u>Lynette Thom</u> <u>David Nicoll</u> please make shareable....its so important...I was trying to find that chemtrail video...you know the ones with the skeletons in it !!!...Somehow l am still able to share far and wide ▯▯▯▯▯David l hope your travelling well ▯What a year huh !!What a lifetime really ▯▯▯♀▯

Travelling?

Ooohh,

I wish!

To go,

Somewhere?

To get away,

From all this

Pish!

All bloody

Rules

And

Regulations,

With no jobs,

Now,

The pubs

Are closed,

No live

Music

Allowed,

Not even

Any singing!

With

Empty

Stands,

At the

Football,

Matches,

The silence,

Ringing!

As we

Get more

Tied down,

With

Bad omens,

And

Pre-Conditioning,

The future,

From our

Politicians,

In the form,

Of more

Lost of

Liberty

And

Freedom,

They

Could

Be

Bringing?

All

In the

Name of

Our

"Health

And

Safety!"

To ruin,

Our

Economy!

To make

Many

Millions,

Rely

On

Universal

Credit?

Or

Furlough

Money?

They are,

The

Lucky ones,

Many,

Are not,

So

Lucky!

As there

Are now,

No jobs

To see!

How does

Anyone now,

Make

Money?

Being led

And

Daily fed,

The

Statistics

Of gloom,

Taking

All the

Attention,

Of the

Masses,

Listening

To false

Projections,

In the

Papers,

Or

On the

TV!

In the

Living room?

Making it

A Big

FEAR!

Enough,

To make

You

Sigh!

Did you

Ever ask

Why?

Face!

The people all still think that it is about the Flu as that is all that is on the TV, constant fear of catching it, even with a 99% survival rate and 99% chance that you wont get it. Heavy reliance on cases, which are positive test results only, even though the people are fine, showing no symptoms of anything. Just told to stay at home for two weeks with no medicine apart from panadol and welome them to track and trace! Where if you go out during the quarantine period, then a 1000 pound fine, you could face!

Fiction!

On

Facebook

And

In

Social

Media

Today,

You

Have,

To be

Careful,

About,

Your use,

Of

Words

And

Diction!

Nowadays,

TRUTH!

Is

Stranger,

Than

Fiction!

Fly free!

Got news

This morning,

Which leaves

My heart

In pain!

My great freind

And

Song creator,

Collaborator,

Mervyn Fuller,

We will never,

See again!

He

Passed away,

Just

Yesterday!

Condolences

To

Taryn,

His wife,

Family

And friends,

In our time,

We made many

Poetic and

Musical

Collaborations,

Although now,

I am

In tears!

In our

Creative phase

We produced

Six CDs,

In the

Space of

Five years!

They are all

Now on

YouTube,

Listed as

Mervyn Fuller

And

David Nicoll,

Please

Have a listen,

As we

All now,

To him,

Say

Cheers!

He would

Phone

From

Time to time,

To have a

Wee blether!

For about

An hour,

Then on

Occasion,

At his place?

Or mine?

We would

Get together!

Our story starts,

By giving him,

A copy of

My first book,

Which he was

Excited about,

Longing to

Take a look!

One month later,

He called me,

We lived over

One thousand,

Kilometres

Apart you see!

"I have made

A song from one

Of your poems!"

He said to me!

Then played it

Over the phone,

So that,

I could hear

And see!

His talent

In

Songwriting

And

Making song,

From

Poetry!

We were

MAD,

Mervyn

And

Dave!

As

Listed on

Each CD!

"Make

Song

Lyrics

About this

................."

He would

Say to me!

Which I

Would do,

Immediately,

He would

Trigger me!

Into action,

With

Creative

Poetry!

These

Triggers,

Are the

Titles

Of all

Of our tracks,

Which were,

In total

Fifty!

To help

Others,

Ultimately!

"They will

Listen,

To the

Track titles,

That they

Resonate with!"

He would say,

To me!

After receiving

The lyrics,

He would then,

Convert them,

Into song!

Being a

Retired,

Singer,

Songwriter

And

Guitarist

Of note,

It would not

Take him,

Too long!

Decide on

The style,

Rock,

Rhythm,

Reggae,

Easy listening?

In musical

Creativity,

He was

Strong!

He would then,

Pull in

His freinds,

Mike Pregnolatu,

On lead guitar,

And

Mike Laatz,

On

Saxophone!

To add

Their

Creative magic,

He was not

On his own!

Now his time,

On this earth

Has flown!

He was a

Spiritual man,

Coming from a

Spiritual family,

Remember

Him saying,

To me!

That

"When

We move on,

We are free!

Moving on

Into the

Realms,

Of

Spirituality!"

It was

A pleasure

And an

Honour,

Knowing

You

Mervyn,

May your

Spirit,

RIP,

Now

You,

Fly free!

With love brother!

THE BEST OF MAD

MERVYN FULLER

DAVID NICOLL

TREAT IT SO !

A POETIC AND MUSICAL COLLABORATION
BY
MERVYN FULLER
AND
DAVID NICOLL

Mervyn fuller
And
David nicoll

THIS IS MAD 2 !
A POETIC AND MUSICAL COLLABORATION

ON DAYS LIKE THESE

Mervyn And David
FULLER   NICOLL
A MUSICAL AND POETIC COLLABORATION

Forgiven!

Like a

Stairway,

To

Heaven,

In

A

Strange,

Kind,

Of

Way,

With

Th e

Rungs,

Going,

Up

And

Away!

They

Cam,e

From

Planes,

That

Flew

By!

And

Left

Them,

In the

Sky!

They

Were

Not even,

Flying,

Very high!

You

Can see

How it

Spreads,

Slowly!

To

Block

Out

The

Sun,

Pretty

Quickly!

While

People,

On the

Ground,

Dont even

Notice them,

Certainly not,

The

Majority!

They never

Look up,

No interest,

Controlled

By the

Telly,

The

BBC!

All

News

And

Statistics,

Things to keep,

In your

Head!

While at night

You

Silently

Dread,

Without

Ever

Noticing,

What is

Going on,

Outside,

Right over,

Your

Own head!

We are being

Geoengineered!

They just

Never said!

No ones

Consent,

Was ever asked,

And none

Was given!

Will

They,

For what,

They are

Doing,

Ever

Be

Forgiven?

Freedom Away!

Temporarily

Banned,

From

Sharing posts

Until

Twenty three,

Twenty

On

Wednesday!

So the sign,

Did say!

Must have

Upset,

The

Thought Police,

Sorry,

Fact Checkers

In some way?

But you

Never know,

Why?

As they,

Dont say!

They just

Give you,

Your

Sentence

And

Take,

Your

Freedom,

Away!

Fuck you!

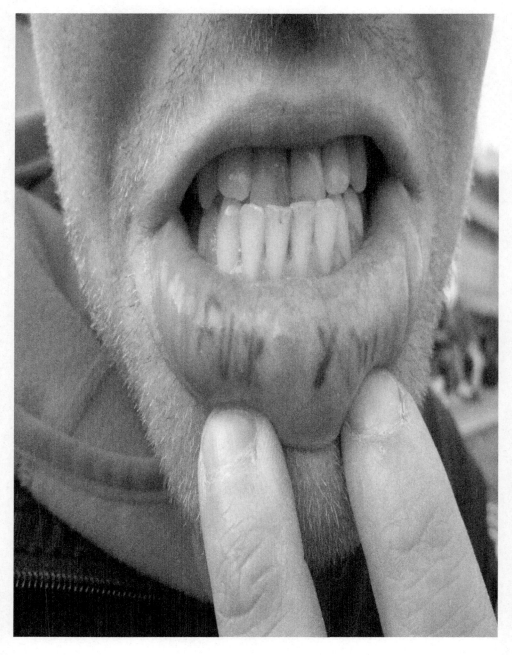

Going Away!

Onlyessential travel is allowed,

"Why are you travelling today?"

"I am travelling for the

Human Rights and Freedom!

Of Humanity!"

Is what I would say!

"To speak with like minded souls,

Who can see,

What is going on today!"

The whole world

Locked Down!

Because of the flu!

Which we have had,

Every single year,

In the winter

With little,

That we could do!

Just isolate

And

Treat the sick,

Hoping that they,

Would pull through!

But now our economy is gone!

Everyone sitting at home,

Very few having fun!

With new laws

And restrictions,

Blocking your freedom

And Liberty

At every turn!

All in the name

Of our

Health and Safety!

When will all the

Draconian laws,

Be rescinded?

That is hard to say!

This whole

Virus smokescreen,

Is globally orchestrated

And Preplanned

In every way!

Look up the

Rockefeller's Lock Step 2010

Document and you can see

In these plans,

Exactly where we stand today!

With Lock Downs being a

Permanent fixture

For many a long day!

With massive fines

Or even jail time?

For those who dont agree,

With what they say!

But,

Here we are

Anyway!

We do not consent!

And we are not,

Going Away!

Goebbels Doctrine!

Quoted by Snooze 2 Awaken:

On this subject it's worth recalling this famous quote by the infamous Nazi propagandist Joseph Goebbels, who would be proud to see world leaders and international mainstream media carrying on his tradition of deceit and control on such an epic scale:

"If you tell a lie big enough and keep repeating it, people will eventually come to believe it. The lie can be maintained only for such time as the State can shield the people from the political, economic and/or military consequences of the lie. It thus becomes vitally important for the State to use all of its powers to repress dissent, for the truth is the mortal enemy of the lie, and thus by extension, the truth is the greatest enemy of the State."

Happening Tomorrow!

Not sure,

If it is,

Old

Age?

Or

Premature

Senility?

Or,

Because

Of the

Imposed,

Never ending,

Lock down?

Every day,

Is the same,

To me!

But tonight,

I went to a

Guy Fawkes,

Lock Down

Protest meeting,

At

Glasgow green

And

When I

Got there,

No people,

Not another

Soul,

Did I see!

The place,

Was

Empty!

Thinking,

Why is

No one,

Here?

I could

Not see!

So instead,

Went for a

Walk about,

To

The Clutha bar,

The outside

Paintings there,

To see!

Got back home,

And on my

Laptop,

What do

I see?

This created

In me!

A mild form

Of

Sorrow!

As the date,

Shown on it,

Was the

Fourth,

Of

November,

The

Meeting,

Is

Actually,

Happening,

Tomorrow!

Happy New FEAR!

Message from the Government:

**We wish you a
Merry Xmas
And a
Happy New FEAR!**

Alternative!

**We wish you a
Merry Xmas
And a
Happy New TIER!**

Head their way!

What should we do to flatten these curbs David?

Go back to work and open up society again without worrying about a flu variant that doesn't even kill that many. Rescind the new Draconian laws that have been put in place, allow people to visit others again including family. Let people do what they used to enjoy doing including playing music.

Be realistic!

What,

Are you really,

Worried about?

Please,

Check out

The

Overall,

Death

Figures,

For the

UK!

And

See,

What it,

Does say?

It says

That,

No

More
People,
Are
Dying
Now,
Than
There,
Were,
Last
Year!
So,
Is
Their,
Really,
A
Pandemic,
Here?
Just
Shows
You,
The
Power
Of
The
MSM
And
TV!

As,

For the

Last nine

Months,

Only

Fear!

Is

All

They

See,

And

Hear!

Daily

Changing

Statistics,

Hitting,

Every

Heart

And

Ear!

Brainwashing

And

Propaganda,

Swallowing!

Think that,

There might,

Be

Something

Afoot,

Here!

Steering,

If

Not

Mandating!

A

New,

Made

B,y

Many

Companies,

Warp speed

Vaccine!

With no

Comeback

On them.

If anything

Goes wrong!

Not,

A

Cool scene!

As the

Government funds

From

Taxpayers

Money,

Has

So far

Paid out,

Over

Four billion,

Dollars,

In the

USA,

For

Vaccine

Injuries,

Quite

Obscene!

The

British public

Have

Not had

This

So far,

But will

Soon learn,

What it,

Does mean!

As the

Corporations

And

Billionaires,

Keep

Rolling

In

The

Green!

With

Mask

Wearing

And

Social

Distancing!

Only

Being

Introduced,

When

The

COVID,

Curve

Was,

Flattening!

The

Following

Curves,

Are

Now

Sky

Rocketing!

Unemployment,

Bankrupcy,

Suicide

Overdoses,

Domestic

And

Child abuse,

Depression,

Starvation,

While

The

Elite,

Many

Things,

Are

Pocketing!

Long white

Spreading

Streaks,

Criss cross

Our skies!

They

Tell us,

That

It,

Is

Contrails,

Which

Is,

Absolute

Lies!

With the

General

Population,

Not

Even

Seeing,

Them,

With

Their,

Own

Eyes!

They

Take

It,

For

Granted

And

From

Cellphones,

Rarely

Raise,

Their

Eyes!

A

New

World

Order,

Takeover,

Is

Underway!

With

Us

All

Under,

House

Arrest,

Not

Allowed,

Out

To

Play!

From

Others,

We

Must

Now,

Stay away!

If you dont,

Then

Massive

And

Doubling,

Fines,

Will

Be

Coming,

Your way!

Maybe even,

They might,

Take you

Away?

Who

Can

Say?

So

Deadly,

Is

The

Story,

Of

This

Flu,

Today!

But,

What

They,

Forget

To say!

Is that,

We have,

Had the

Flu here,

Since the

First

Scotsman,

Arrived here,

Every winter,

Sure,

It took

Some away!

But life

Went on

Day to day!

Without

Shutting down,

Everything,

To try

To make

It,

Go away!

This

Lock Down

Is far

More

Damaging

To us,

Than any

Flu virus,

That is

Going

Around,

Today!

Can you

See

Through,

The

Smokescreen,

Yet?

I

Do

Hope so,

Is

What,

I

Say!

If not,

From

Now on,

You

Will be

Taking,

RNA

Modifying

And

Possibly

Sterilising?

Injections

Yearly,

To

Keep,

The

New

Variant,

Away!

Do

You,

Want it

That way?

If

So,

Then

OK!

If

You

Dont

And

Would like,

Like minds,

To see!

Find out,

Who,

Your

Local

Lock Down

Protest

Group

Is

And

Head

Their

Way!

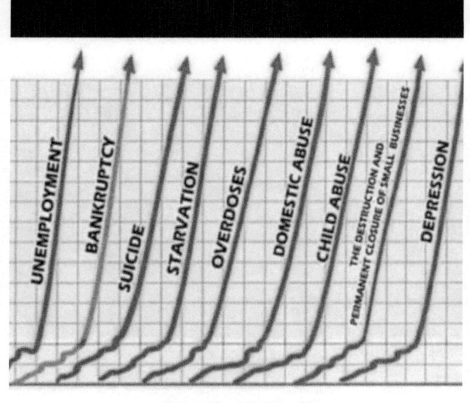

2020

Who's going to flatten these curves?

Heavens Way?

Today,

Will go

Down,

In

History!

The

Eighth of

December

2020!

The day when

In the UK,

The vaccinations,

Started

To supposedly,

Save

Makind

From

COVID!

Whether,

Or not?

That it

Actually will,

Well,

That,

In the

Long term,

We

Shall see!

It starts,

In the

Care

Homes

With

The

Over

Eighty!

Who have

No say in this,

For them,

It is

Compulsory!

So,

Right at

This moment,

They are

Injecting,

Many peoples,

Father,

Mother,

Grandad,

Or

Granny?

Will it

Shorten

Their lives?

Or have

Some other

Adverse

Effects?

Well,

Very soon,

We shall see!

Why do the

Government

Need an

AI system,

To handle calls,

From consumers

Affected

In this

Nation?

Are they

Expecting,

A

Tsunami?

Only

Nine months ago,

We were

Still free!

There was

No sign here,

Of any

Alien

Virus,

Which now,

Leaves us all

With a frown!

As because

Of its

Appearance,

Since last

March,

We have

All been,

In our

Own homes.

Self imprisoned

And

Locked down!

Our businesses

And jobs

Now gone,

No more vibrant

Economy!

With millions

On

Universal credit

Or

Furlough

Money!

Only

Hardship now,

Massive

Unemployment

And

Poverty!

With great

Fear,

Being spread,

Globally!

Manipulated,

Inflated,

Death statistics,

And

Now cases,

Streaking upwards,

In graphs,

Shown on

Every TV!

All around

The whole world,

People are

All captured,

In this

Manufactured

And well planned

Operation!

Unfortunately!

With

Bill (God) Gates

And his vaccine

Company

Owned mates,

Hitting overtime

Big time,

To get them,

Delivered

In

Crates!

At minus

Seventy degrees!

Will this bring,

Humanity,

To its

Knees?

Will

Billions

Possibly

Be

Needing

Gravestones,

To stand

In the

Chilly breeze?

Never before

Has such

Speed been seen!

From the

Emergence

Of the virus,

To an

Approved

Vaccine!

In less that

Twelve months?

Without animal

Testing!

Many,

Many people

Wondering!

About this

Whole set up

From

Event 201s

Pre Planning

To Vaccine

Distributing!

With immunity

Granted

To the

Manufacturers,

Such a

Crazy scene!

With over

Four Billion

Dollars already

Paid out,

For injuries in

The USA!

That

Sucks

Quite a bit,

Know what

I mean?

With

Autism,

Now becoming

Commonplace,

Whereas

Before,

It was,

Rarely,

Seen!

Not long now

Until

Xmas day!

Lets see,

How many

Peoples lives,

Have been

Affected

By it,

In any way?

Or

Since

The

injections,

They

Have now,

Gone

Heavens,

Way?

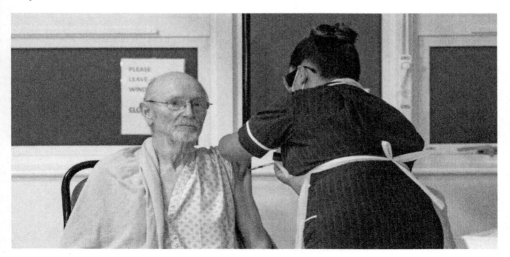

History!

Rudolf Steiner

Warned us,

At

The

Turn,

Of

The

Century!

As

If,

In

Prophecy,

"Sometime,

In

The

Future,

Dark forces

Will come

Into,

A

Mans

Heart

And

Via

An

Injection,

He

Will

Cut

Off,

Mans

Link,

To

God,

Or

Spirituality!

At

That

Time,

Unbeleivable,

But

Now?

Is

It,

Almost

A

Reality?

As

A

Video,

Shows,

A

Young

Bill Gates,

Explaining,

To the CIA,

How

An

Injection,

Could

Affect,

A

Persons,

Religious

Extremism,

Co incidentaly!

The same

Person,

Who

Pushes

Us

Now,

To

"The

Whole

Population,

Of

The

Planet,

Must be

Vaccinated,

If they

Wish,

Once

Again,

To

Be

Free!"

He

Seems

To

Now

Be,

A

Global

Authority!

On

Everyones

Health

And

Safety!

By

Making

These

Things

Mandatory!

Him

Coming,

From

Eugenists,

His

Family!

Who

Seek,

A

Massive

Decrease,

In

Numbers,

On this

Beautiful,

Earth,

Of

Humanity!

Which

Seems,

Like

A

Bit,

Of

A

Polar

Opposite!

To me!

Everything

He

Does,

He

Does

It,

For

Money!

With

A

Twenty,

To

One,

Return,

On

Vaccines,

He

Will

Be

Obscenely

Wealthy!

As he,

Has

Invested,

In the

Seven

Main,

Vaccine

Makers,

Inevitably!

Killing

Two

Birds,

With

One

Stone?

We

Might

Well

See?

Looking

Back,

On

Our

Present

Time,

When

It,

Becomes,

History!

Dr. Rudolf Steiner, Christian Mystic & Clairvoyant, founder Waldorf Schools

I have told you that the spirits of darkness are going to inspire their human hosts, in whom they will be dwelling, to find a vaccine that will drive all inclination towards spirituality out of people's souls when they are very young - Dr. Rudolf Steiner

If you do!

Everybodys

Shit scared,

About,

A

Flu!

Just

Goes to,

Show you!

What

The

Power,

Of

The

MSM

And

TV

Can do!

As,

There

Is,

A

99%

Chance,

That

You,

Won't

Catch it,

And

A

99%

Recovery

Rate,

Even

If,

You

Do!

Indians here!

Walking through

Asda the other day,

Then I hear,

"Don't you see

The arrows?"

A lady

Screamed,

From

Quite far away!

This gave me

A big shock!

Heart

Pounding!

Not in

Good cheer!

Then

Shouted back!

"I

Didn't

Even see,

Any

Indians here!"

Into you!

Went by

The most

Famous shop.

In

Scotland,

Today!

Owned by

Neanie Scott,

In the

High Street,

Of

Edinburgh,

But,

It

Was

Locked,

She

Was

Away!

Thought

That I

Should leave

Her my card!

Couldnt leave

Her any money,

At that time,

But thought,

I will write

Her a poem,

Sometime,

As

I

Am,

After

All,

A

Bard!

Just

Five

Minutes

Later,

Who do

I see?

None other than,

Neanie Scott,

Personally!

Must have

Been,

Destiny!

Good

On you

Neanie,

For making

Your stand!

With no man

Around you,

At that time,

To hold,

Your hand,

You told

Your truth,

Plain

And

True!

To the

Three

Boys in Blue!

Who were

Hassling you!

For doing,

What you do!

We are

Caught,

In

A

Tsunami,

Of

New

Rules

And

Regulations,

Supposedly,

All

About,

The

Flu!

But

You know,

As well

As I do!

That this,

Is not

True!

Our

Freedoms,

Have been

Stripped away,

Our

Economy,

Is

Now,

Buggered,

Too!

So

Great,

To have

Bumped,

Into you!

Ionisation!

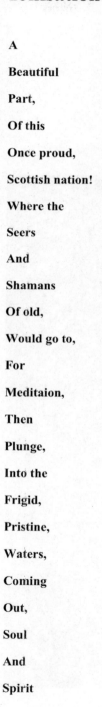

A

Beautiful

Part,

Of this

Once proud,

Scottish nation!

Where the

Seers

And

Shamans

Of old,

Would go to,

For

Meditaion,

Then

Plunge,

Into the

Frigid,

Pristine,

Waters,

Coming

Out,

Soul

And

Spirit

Charged!

In

A

State,

Of

Negative,

Ionisation!

Job!

"Are

Ye

Lookin

Fir

Wirk,

Shuggie?

Tae

Mak,

A

Cuppla,

Bob!"

"Naw,

Ahm,

Nae

Looking,

Fir

Wirk,

But

Ah,

Sur

Cud

Dae,

Wi

A

Job!

Laboratory!

Always

Special

Skyscapes,

You have,

On that

Side,

Emory.

Like

A

Geoengineering

Laboratory!

Longer free!

Would love that Michael or post them here? davidrbnicoll@gmail.com Do you know that there are a lot of great poets in SMAAPP? We did an Anthology last year called A case for Humanity Vol 1! Haven't played much since coming back here, living in a first floor flat, comfy but you just dont get too many djembe players around here! The times when I did play they loved it though and had not heard anything like it before. Finished off a book launch with The wildlife at the Zoo! Quite a heavy rhythm and sudden end!

Also in the Clutha bar with my mate Bert on percussion.

What Lock Down rules and regs. do you have you there?

I have been writing constantly through the "spend more time at home" phase since last March. Just released a new book recently. Scottish Thoughts and Reflections Vol 4!Now doing poetry at Lock Down protest meetings in different cities and towns in Scotland.

Used to

Write,

About

Wildlife,

Now it's

More,

About

Humanity!

And the

Lock Down,

Globaly

Imposed,

Insanity!

Creating,

Mass

Unemployment

And

Poverty!

The

NHS,

Is

As

Good,

As

Gone,

Unless,

You

Have,

Covid?

We

Are,

Living

Under,

Ever

Changing,

Rules

And

Regulations,

With

Fines,

Or

Jail

Time?

For

Harming

No one,

Stealing

Nothing,

No

Victim,

No

Crime,

Feeding

The

Corporation's

Lust,

Ultimately!

And

Now,

We

Are

No

Longer

Free!

MANIFEST

When seeking inspiration
For something new,
One has to go inside
To find out what to do,
For the inspiration
Is from the spirit
Who inspires
And guides
You through!

When dreaming of the future,
Of things you would like to be,
Your thoughts amass,
Then fly out,
Into universal energy!
Time ticks by whether
At work or at rest,
Until your dream
Becomes.....
Manifest!

Mind Unfortunately!

The

Mask

Wearing

Scenario,

Was

Introduced

When

The

Curve flattened

You know!

But now,

With the

Fear,

No one,

Is in,

Good

Cheer!

Around

Other people,

They steer!

Dont want

Anyone near!

Over

The

Top,

Of

The

Masks,

They peer!

Without knowing,

That not enough

Oxygen

Is

Reaching

Your body!

Which will

In time,

Bring illness,

Undoubtedly!

Even though

They,

Have

Made

It

Mandatory!

It

Blinkers,

The

Mind

Unfortunately!

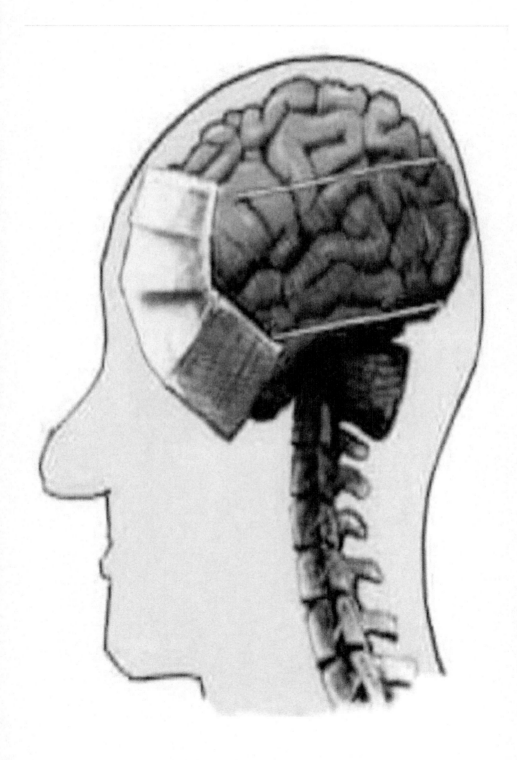

Morningmare!

Sometimes,

After

Waking,

Into

Space,

You

Stare!

With

Having,

A

Second

Sleep,

Just

Realised,

That,

I

Had,

A

Morningmare!

Musical Symphony!

Just had a call,

From a friend

In South Africa,

To tell of a

Mutual friend,

Of ours called

Mervyn Fuller's

Moving on!

He had

Emphysema,

For many years,

It is

Cannabis oil,

That kept

Him alive,

I know,

He told me,

That it,

Was

Not fun!

Mervyn and I

Were creators,

In a poetical

And musical team!

He would ask me,

To write lyrics

For subjects,

Then make them

Into a song!

Usually

Within a month,

A lyricists dream!

Superb sounds,

I must say!

Please listen to them,

Whatever track titles,

That you resonate with,

Then,

On YouTube,

You can play!

He had been

Suffering

From the

Emphysema,

For manys a day!

The Cannabis oil,

Kept the effects,

Of it away!

We lived

Mervyn!

Maybe the

Last generation,

Of people,

Who were

Free?

Not like

Nowadays,

Where your

Family

And friends,

In other houses,

You cannot see!

With the

Great majority,

Taking their

Instructions

Daily,

From,

In the UK,

The ever present,

Always on,

Programming,

Listening,

And recording

Smart TV!

So glad,

That we,

Were

MAD!

(Mervyn And Dave!)

Brought

Together,

By

Destiny!

Hopefully,

Some hearts

And

Minds,

We will,

Set free!

When they

Listen,

To our,

Poetic

And

Musical

Symphony!

Narrative Blindly!

Well,

Here are

The facts,

Stated

Plainly!

It is

Such,

A

Pity,

That

It,

Is

Not

Understood,

By

The

Majority!

Who

Follow,

The

Mainstream

Narrative,

Blindly!

‼️ THE RAW TRUTH OF OUR REALITY ⚠️

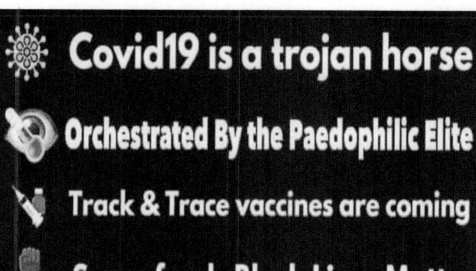

Covid19 is a trojan horse

Orchestrated By the Paedophilic Elite

Track & Trace vaccines are coming

Soros funds Black Lives Matter

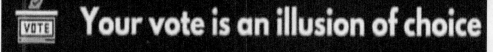

Your vote is an illusion of choice

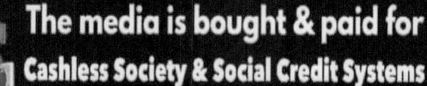

The media is bought & paid for

Cashless Society & Social Credit Systems are Coming

Masks are a sign of your compliance

STAND UP FOR THE TRUTH

New World To See!

Howling

To the

Moon!

The

Wolf,

In his prime!

While his family,

Sit on the

High Point,

Surveying,

Their

Territory!

Relaxing,

At a

Peaceful

Moment in time!

Far away

From winter chills,

Above the

Assegay valley,

In

KwaZuluNatal,

South Africa,

In the

Valley,

Of

1000 hills!

Around

My old home,

The Irie Eyrie,

They did roam!

Socialising,

Playing,

Breeding,

Never

Being,

On my own,

Digging tunnels,

To have

Their young,

As Snow

The

Pure white

Artic Wolf

Female digs,

In heavily

Sloping ground,

Beneath

A bush

For cover,

The entrance

Is found!

With

Loose scree,

And earth,

Spread

All around!

The tunnel,

Low

And

Curving

Round!

Then she

Goes in,

Pushes loose

Earth in

Front of her,

Her eyes

Through

A

Slit

Of

Torchlight

You see!

She stays

There

For

Four days,

To give

Birth

And

Succle,

Her new

Family!

Four weeks

Later,

These

Wee furry,

Beautiful

Wolves,

Come out,

The

Brand

New

World

To see!

No Girls!

This really

Never

Gave anyone,

Any

Good cheer!

When

We got

Told,

That

We can

Go back

To the pub,

But we,

Are not

Allowed,

To buy

Any beer!

What on earth,

Is this?

Where now,

Will we get

Our thrills?

Its

Like

Saying,

It is

OK,

To

Enter,

The

Brothel,

But,

There

Are,

No

Girls!

Of Humanity!

Let me

Introduce

You

To

Mark Steele!

He has

Formed

SUN,

Save Us Now!

Political

Activist,

Party!

He is

An

Expert,

In

60 Ghz mm

Microwave,

Technology,

That is now

Buzzing,

Around us,

Wherever,

We may be,

In the

Whole

Country,

Even

Transmitting from

Many sattelites,

Beaming

On

Land

And

From

The

Air,

Constantly!

All

Part,

Of

The

New

World

Order,

You see?

With new

Diseases,

With

Unknown

Causes,

Being

Labelled

As

"Kawasaki!"

He

Tells

The

Truth!

Which

The

Powers

That be!

Do

Not

Like,

Funnily!

Then

They,

Act

Accordingly,

By

Removing him,

From

All

The

Social,

Platforms,

Including

YouTube,

Trying to

Silence him,

So that he,

Is not

Heard,

By the

Majority!

"These

Pink

Blotches,

In the skin,

That people

Are getting,

Is

Radiation

Poisoning!"

Said he!

That

Answers

The question,

But not suitable

Information,

To go out

To the masses,

Who are

Being led along,

Blindly!

So scared

Of getting,

And

Dying

From

C-V-D!

All

Brainwashed

And

Programmed,

By the

TV!

Spreading

Its

Fear

And

Statistics daily,

Beaming

Straight,

Into

The

Left brain,

Immediately!

He does not

Mince

His words

"It is a

Military

Grade

Battlefield

Weapon!"

Said he!

This new

60GHz mm

Microwave,

Technology!

Installed

During

Lock Down,

Quickly

And

Quietly!

Check

Out

The

Lampost,

Outside

Your

House?

Is it

Flat

on

The

Bottom,

With

A

Transmitter,

On

Top?

Welcome

To

The

IOT!

He

Will

Not,

Be

Silenced,

You

Will

See!

As

He,

Is

Speaking,

For

The

Betterment,

And

Saving

Of

Humanity!

On the Flu!

It is

Xmas eve

In Stornoway!

The people

Are out

And

Where

They can,

Are in bars

To talk

And play!

But,

Life,

Changes

Here,

On

Boxing day!

This will

Not lead,

To any

Good cheer!

As on

That day,

They move

Into

Another

Tier!

Then

The

Bars,

Will

Be

Closed

Up here!

Same

As

It has

Been in

Glasgow,

For

Many

A

Day!

It

Removes,

A

Big part

Of

Socialising,

In

Many

A way!

The

Government,

Just want

You,

At home,

To stay!

Can

You see?

That

This,

Is

Not,

OK?

Them,

Laying

Down

The

Rules,

Seemingly

Little,

That you,

Can do?

Wanting

You,

To get the

Mandatory

Injections,

Severe

Lock Downs,

Social distancing,

Mask wearing,

Imposed

Social isolation,

Everyone,

Living in

Fear,

Unemployment,

Suicidal,

With

Frustration,

Listening

To

The

Evening news,

And

Getting

Programmed

And

Instructed,

Each

And

Every day!

And

Them

Saying,

It

Is

For

Our

Health

And

Safety!

The

Governments

Ruling

The roost,

With

Impunity!

With

Self given

Powers

Due to a

Convenient

PLANNEDemic

Emergency!

Laying down

The laws,

Restricting our

Freedoms,

Extremely

Dramatically!

With fines

For breaking

These new laws,

Doubling up

Consequently,

To

A

Maximum

Of

In

Pounds

Nine

Hundred

And

Sixty!

Is

It

Not,

Ironic?

The

Economy,

Deliberately!

Being

Destroyed,

Is on the

Way out,

As our

Normal

Lives are,

Dear God

Help us

Through!

They are

Blaming,

It all,

On the flu!

One Fifty!"

At an

Auction in Glasgow,

An American buyer

Lost his wallet,

Carrying

Ten thousand pound!

He could not find it,

It was not around!

"I will give

To the finder of it!

One hundred pound!"

He announced,

To all around!

These

Auctions halls,

Are

Very

Thrifty!

When

A

Scottish

Voice,

From

The

Back,

Of

The

Hall,

Shouted,

"I

Will

Give

Him,

One Fifty!"

Oot!

A

Thoughtful

Scotsman,

Is heading

Doon tae

The pub!

Put your

Hat

And coat,

On love!"

"Ooh,

Are you taking

Me out,

To the pub

As well?"

Is the question,

He wife

Did tell!

"No!"

He said!

As he

Pulled on,

The one boot!

"Its jist that,

Ah want

Tae turn,

The central,

Heatin aff ,

When

Ahm,

Oot!"

Other Yin!

Two

Posters,

Ootside

A

Kirk,

In

Arbroath!

Put

Jimmys

Heid,

In

A

Spin!

The

One

Said,

"Drink

Is

Your

Enemy!"

And

"Love

Your

Enemy!"

On The Other Yin!

Our History!

Headline:

Ontario's Chief Medical Officer of Health

Caught admitting that she just

Says whatever they

Tell her to.

Then going on to say that even if you get the vaccine

You could still transmit it and catch it.

Momo Clark

Wowwww 🙈🙈🙊

David Nicoll

All script readers the lot of them. Bet she regrets that wee slip of the tounge after listening to what she said after that. Life is a stage old William Shakespeare the 1st said.

Rob Preston

"I never look at them, I just read whatever they put in front of me"

"Even when vaccinated you can still be a symptomatic and pass on the disease, so you still have to protect yourself and others"

WHAT'S IT GONNA TAKE 🙈🙈🙈

David Nicoll

When is

Mankind,

Going

To

Stop

Wearing

Masks

And

Killing

Themselves?

By

Doing

So!

As

Not

Enough

Oxygen,

To

Their

Body

And

Brain,

Does

Flow!

They

Will

Get

Sick,

It is,

Just

That,

At the

Moment,

This fact,

They,

Do

Not know!

It is,

Insanity!

That,

The

Authority!

Has

Mandated,

It

To

Be!

It is,

In the

Psyche now,

The

Fear,

The

Distrust,

Imposed,

On all

People,

Globally!

Much

More,

To this,

Than

The

Eye,

Can

See!

As

Will

Be,

Taught,

In

Our,

History!

Plans!

UN Agenda 21/2030 Mission Goals

One World Government
One World cashless Currency
One World Central Bank
One World Military
The end of national sovereignty
The end of ALL privately owned property
The end of the family unit
Depopulation, control of population growth and population density
Mandatory multiple vaccines
Universal basic income (austerity)
Microchipped society for purchasing, travel, tracking and controlling
Implementation of a world Social Credit System (like China has)
Trillions of appliances hooked into the 5G monitoring system (Internet of Things)
Government raised children
Government owned and controlled schools, Colleges, Universities
The end of private transportation, owning cars, etc.
All businesses owned by government/corporations
The restriction of nonessential air travel
Human beings concentrated into human settlement zones, cities
The end of irrigation
The end of private farms and grazing livestock
The end of single family homes
Restricted land use that serves human needs
The ban of natural non synthetic drugs and naturopathic medicine
The end of fossil fuels

👍😠 5   1 Comment

Previously?

Martin Macleod:

Some truth's there alright. Im surrounded by sheeple here. everyone is brainwashed by constant repetition from mainstream media. i dont dare voice my actual opinions for fear of upsetting some family members. nobody willing to consider that the endless lockdowns are doing more harm than good.

David Nicoll:

Yeah to discuss radical matter up there leaves you a bit ostracised, was talking to people there are well to try to enlighten them but the TV and its programming in sacrosanct there. a good way to get through to them is this.

We have had

The flu here

Every year!

Since the coves

Started building

The Callanish stones!

We used to

Isolate the sick,

Then they either

Recovered,

Or

Turned to

Skin and bones?

We never

Shut the

Economy!

We never

Told everyone,

To stay at home,

That would be,

Insanity!

As everyone,

Had to get on,

With their lives,

You see!

But

This year!

Everyone,

Is full of

FEAR!

Getting

Their

Information

And

Instructions,

From the

TV!

As the

Elderly,

For ten months now,

Have been

Living in

Care homes,

In

Solitary!

Where you are

Not even allowed,

To visit

Your friends,

Or

Family?

Most businesses

Now closed

Compulsory!

With new

Untested vaccines,

About to

Become,

Mandatory!

This is

Not just

Happening,

Locally,

But also

Globally!

With anyone

Questioning,

The official

Narrative,

Being

Classified as

C-V-D deniers,

Or

Coronavirus sceptics?

Unfortunately!

 A New

World

Order,

Or

One

World

Government?

Is moving in

Surrepticiously!

And

Secretly!

As through

The course of

This year,

This,

Will become,

More plain,

To see!

Mask wearing

And

Social

Distancing,

Being a

Massive

Psychological

Operation!

Played on

Humanity!

Whilst

Millions of

Children,

Go

Missing each year!

No more of them,

Do we,

Ever see!

With

Bill (God) Gates

Being involved

In it,

From a to Z!

This could be,

The end times,

As stated

In

Biblical

Texts,

Previously?

Question to me?

"Please,

Join

Our

Party

And

Be,

An

MP!"

"Do

You

Know,

That

You,

Are

The

Third,

Person,

To ask,

The

Same

Question,

To me?"

React?

Now

Theres

A

Good idea,

How come,

No one,

Has thought,

About that?

While

The

Children,

Continue,

To

Go

Missing,

Without

Being,

Found,

Does

That

Fact!

Not

Make,

You

React?

Rest!

"Must

Take

These,

New

Trousers

Back!

This,

Is

Not

Fun!"

I

Told

Mark,

My

Eldest,

Son!

" I

Really

Like them,

A

Straight

Black,

Thought,

That

They,

Were

The

Best!

But

It

Looks,

Like

They,

Have

Shrunk,

In

The

Wash,

Just

Like,

All

The

Rest!"

Rockefeller Lockstep 2010

Was Blueprint for 2020 COVID-19 Pandemic

Excerpt from Thomas Williams THI Special Exposé Part 2:

"Do you want to know what lies in store for us? Here it is!"

The Covid-Plan / Rockefeller Lockstep 2010

They hypothesize a simulated global outbreak required steps, various phases, overall timelines, and expected outcomes. This was posited in the Rockefeller Lockstep 2010:

Create a very contagious but super low mortality rate virus to fit the needed plan. Using SARS, HIV, Hybrid Research Strain created at Fort Dietrich Class 4 lab from 2008 to 2013 as part of a research project to find out why corona viruses spread like wildfire in bats but have an extremely hard time infecting humans. To counteract that, they added 4 HIV inserts into the virus. The missing key to infect the human is the Ace-2-Receptor.

Create a weaponized version of the virus with a much higher mortality rate as a backup plan. Ready to be released in Phase 3, but only if needed. SARS, HIV, MERS, Weaponized Tribit Strain created at Fort Dietrich Class 4 lab in 2015.

Transport the Research Strain to different Class 4 lab, the National Microbiology Lab in Winnipeg Canada, and have it "stolen and smuggled out by China", Xi Jang Lee, on purpose and taken to China's only Class 4 lab which is Wuhan Institute of Virology in Wuhan China. For added plausible deniability and to help cement the wanted backup public script as something to fall back on if needed. The primary script being its natural. Backup script being that China created it and released it by accident.

Fund all the talking heads: Fauci, Birx, Tedros and agencies, World Health Organization, NIAID, the CDC and also the UN, that would be involved with pandemic response prior to the planned release of the Research Strain to control the wanted script throughout the operation.

Create and fund the vaccination development and roll out plan so it's capable of being rolled out on a global scale. Gates: A Decade of Vaccines and the Global Action Vaccine action plan, 2010 to 2020.

Create and fund the vaccination, verification and certification protocols, Digital ID, to enforce/confirm the vaccination program after the mandatory roll out is enacted. Gates: ID2020.

Simulate the lockstep hypothesis just prior to the planned Research Strain release using a real-world exercise as a final war game to determine expected response, timelines, and outcomes, Event 201 in Oct 2019.

Release the Research Strain at the Wuhan Institute of Virology itself and then blame its release on a natural scapegoat as the wanted primary script. Wuhan wet market, Nov 2019. Exactly the same as the simulation.

Downplay the human-to-human transmission for as long as possible to allow the Research Strain to spread on a global scale before any country can lock down respond to avoid initial infection.

Once a country has seen infection in place, lock down incoming/outgoing travel. Keep the transmission within the country spreading for as long as possible.

Once enough people in a country/ region are infected, enact forced quarantines/isolation for that area and expand the lockdown regions slowly over time

Overhype the mortality rate by tying the Research Strain to deaths that have little to nothing to do with the actual virus to keep the fear and compliance at a maximum. If anyone dies for any reason and is found to have Covid, consider it a Covid death. And if anyone is thought to of maybe had symptoms of Covid, assume they have Covid, and consider it as a Covid death.

Keep the public quarantines for as long as possible to destroy the region's economy, create civil unrest, break down the supply chain, and cause the start of mass food shortages. As well as cause people's immune system to weaken due to a lack of interaction with other people's bacteria, the outside world, aka the things that keep our immune systems alert and active.

Downplay and attack any potential treatments and continue to echo that the only cure that is viable to fight this virus is the vaccine.

Continue to drag out the quarantine over and over again in "two-week intervals" [There is that two weeks spell casting again. It is a CIA program.] causing more and more people to eventually stand up and protest. Defy them.

[And here is the key part to now:] Eventually end Phase 1 quarantine once they get enough public push back, expected June 2020, and publicly state that they think it's "too early to end the isolation, but I'm going to do it anyways."

Once the public go back to normal, wait a few weeks and continue to overhype the Research Strain mortality rate, Aug to Sept 2020, and combine it with the increase in deaths due to people dying from standard illnesses at a higher rate than normal due to having highly weakened immune systems from months of being in isolation [Which backs up what I said: you should social-distance people who wear masks regular. That's what they've just told you. They have highly weakened immune systems.] to help further pad the mortality rate and also hype the up and coming Phase 2 lockdown.

We are here at the moment:

Eventually, enact Phase 2 quarantines, Oct through Nov 2020, on an even more extreme level and blame the protesters, mostly people who don't trust their governments already, as the cause of the largest second wave whereby the media will say 'we told you so. It was too early. It's all your own fault because you needed a haircut. Your freedoms have consequences.' [Should this all unfold in this manner, the US election will be cancelled delayed or suspended. My opinion. How can you vote with Phase 2 quarantines? You can't.]

Enforce the Phase 2 quarantines at a much more extreme level increasing the penalty for defiance. Replace fines with jail time. Deem all travel as non-essential. Increase checkpoints, including military assistance. Increase tracking/tracing after population via mandatory app. Take over control of food, gas, and create large scale shortages so that people can only get access to essential products or services if they are first given permission.

Keep the Phase 2 lockdown in place for a much longer period of time than the Phase 1 lockdown, continuing to destroy the global economy. Further degrade the supply chain and further amplify the food shortages and the like. Quell any public outrage using extreme actions or force and make anyone who defies them appear as public enemy #1 to those who are willing to submit.

After a rather long Phase 2 lockdown of 6 months plus, roll out the vaccination program and the vaccine certification and make it mandatory for everyone, giving priority access to those that submitted from the start and have those that are for it attack those that are against it, saying 'they are a threat and the cause of all the problems' by using words like "We can't go back to normal until everyone takes the vaccine." And people defying them are "hurting our way of life and therefore are the enemy." [In other words they are going to turn the people against each other.]

If the majority of people go along with the agenda, then let those people enter the new system, the new normal, while limiting the minority that defied the agenda's ability to work, travel and live.

If the majority of people go against the agenda, then release the Weaponized SARS/HIV/MERS Tribit Strain as a Phase 3 operation. A virus with a 30+% mortality rate as a final scare to punish the minority to quickly become the majority and give a final "We told you so" to those that didn't listen.

Enact the new economy model. Microsoft patent 060606 crypto currency system using body activity data which is based on human behavior and willingness to submit. It is a tweaked version of the black mirrors 15 million merits program using food, water, shelter, and other essentials as a weapon of enforcement of the new economic system. Basically, do what we want and get rewarded. Gain credits score and gain more access to things you need to survive. Or go against what we want and get penalized. Lose credits score and lose access to things you need to survive.

And that is your New World Order: technology on steroids where you have no option but to comply. And if anyone thinks that this isn't true, then go and check out some parts of China because they've already started some of the crypto currencies system in place in certain areas.

So, this is the outline of their plan. And what we have to stop by outing it in as many places as possible. And also calling out Q and Trump and asking them: Are you going to stop this? Mass arrests are irrelevant. This is essential and this has to be blocked.

I have converted this into poetry in the poem titled BC!

Sacred Cow!

Twelve months ago, we were free! Life was normal, used to do, what we wanted, when we wanted, with who we wanted, in Harmony! Live bands in the pubs, great restaurants and friends we would see, used to visit our family, go to the care homes to see Grandad and Granny! Working hard to put food on the table, for our family!

Go on holiday, Anywhere! Or a cruise in the Mediterranean sea? Since then, we have been introduced to an unseen and overhyped virus known as C_V_D! Which has been on just about every death certificate since last March from what we see! Hospitals seemingly empty! Lock Down the Economy! Self isolation and house arrest since then, continuously! People not getting their vitamin D, to keep their immune systems healthy! With Geoengineering planes criss crossing the sky extremely, frequently! That hardly anyone does see! Too busy watching TV! Not believing what they see! Thinking that normal people who dont wear masks are now the enemy! "You are selfish, you could kill someone's Granny!" Neighbours grassing on neighbours, if any breaches of the new laws, they see! The boys in blue reacting immediately and forcefully! What has become now of our society? Brought about by Government laws, given in a state of Emergency! Where some people want to be, locked up, for Eternity? Which Coincidentally, it might just be? Now we have jags in the arms, moving towards becoming Mandatory, creating divide and rule once more between the population ultimately! Can anyone see? That this was preplanned in Event 201, step by step, a rehearsal for reality! Which just six weeks later came to be! What also happened in that time, was the rapid installation of 60GHz mm Microwave technology! Whose cumulative effects are respiratory! And will no doubt be added to the tally statistically!

Because of a flu virus, they have destroyed our economy and all in the name of our Health and Safety! Politicians still happy, as they have not missed one very stuffed wage packet through this whole Emergency!

Just changing our rules and restrictions almost daily! With daily breifings being delivered statistically! Often mind bogglingly! Stay at Home being the order of the day enendingly! But now some people, through the smoke they see! Knowingly, that this is a global operation not done lovingly, for control and power over Humanity, to drive us into hybridisation with AI under a Monopoly! When again,will they ever, open our bars? Elon Musk knows, that the shit, is about to hit the fan, that is why he is planning, on going to Mars! Is their any such thing anymore as a Sacred cow? Please people, look at where we used to be and where we are now!

©HowStuffWorks.com

Sale Anyway!

Hi Dave O'McBrave.

Sorry call ended abruptly last night. Ran FNB battery flat.

You gotta get the hell out of there asap.

Here's my plan for u:

1. Pack all your stuff there (don't know what u got there to pack)

2. Buy one-way ticket to SA, OR Tambo, Jhb. If u have to buy return, get refund for return. Do you have residence permit for SA?

3. I am expecting successful purchase of yr H'crest property.

4. If so, have delivery of your stuff to H'crest. If transfer not complete, have delivery of yr stuff to my Benoni home: 6 Olienhout St, Northvilla, Benoni 1501.

5. Will pick u up @ Tambo. May spend a night or 2 @ my Benoni home.

6. Bring u out to my Tz property, then take u to H'crest on registration (occupation) of that property. Not that far from here, go through Mpumalanga to KZN.

7. The deed is done. Welcome home. The pipe's a-playing, the drums a'drumming.

Get out now whilst u can. Otherwise walk!

Thank you

So much

Claude!

I don't know

What to say!

Absolutely

Delighted,

That you

See things,

That way!

I am

Fighting a battle

Here in Scotland,

As they,

Are taking

Our

Freedom away!

We have been

Locked up,

In our

Own homes

For manys

A day!

We are not

Allowed to move,

From there,

Far away!

It is

Shit!

I must say!

Would dearly love,

To move back

To Africa,

One day!

Buy

The Irie Eyrie

Anyway!

It was designed

For self sufficiency

In every way!

With an

Orchard

And

Food growing

Spirals

Hen shed,

AquaPonics

System,

And all sorts

Of additions,

To keep hunger

At bay,

To make sure,

That you,

Will be

Ok!

Twenty five

Thousand litres,

Of

Stormwater

Storage,

To keep thirst,

From the plants,

Away!

It is

Winter

Up here now,

It is

Cold and grey!

My skin colour

Now

Peely Wally,

Not very

Impressive,

I must say!

Let me know

How it goes

With the

Sale

Anyway!

Secretly!

Strange how
New imposed laws,
Are not very sweet!
Because travelling,
Has now
Been banned,
I felt in
Inverness
Like a criminal
In the street!
Leaving the
Bus station,
I could not
Understand,
Why I felt
Uneasy?
As
Behind me
Was a
Big black,
Trolley case,
In my hand!
And this
Is in,
My own
Birthplace
Of
Scotland!
What on earth
Is going on here?
What can we do?
It seems that
The whole world
And its economy,
Is shut down
And all because
Of the flu?
How can this
Possibly
Be true?

We have had
The flu here,
For many
Thousands,
A year!
You just
Used to isolate
The sick ones!
And carry on
Doing
Whatever,
That
You had
To do!
Life always
Went on,
As we saw,
Each other
Through!
Helping
Each other,
As small
Communities do!
But now,
The government,
Has declared
A Pandemic,
Giving them,
Emergency powers!
To impose
Draconian laws,
Say what we can
And cannot do!
They have
Basically
Taken away,
The freedom,
Of me
And you!
Now very little,
Than we can do!
No work,
No visiting,
Mask wearing,

Social distancing,
No travelling,
Stay at home
They say!
And all of this,
For a flu,
That doesn't
Even kill
That many,
Anyway!
Check out
The overall death
Statistics for the UK
And you will see,
That this
Is true!
No more are
Dying now,
So why
The fear?
That is being
Spread on
The MSM
And TV
Daily!
Making the
Population
Nervous,
In
Anxiety!
Lock downs
Proclaimed,
In the
Whole country!
Where limited
Interactions,
With others
In promoted,
Vigorously!
Suicides
Increasing
Greatly!
As well
As,

Unemployment
And
Small businesses
Bankruptcy!
All the
Bars closed,
Your friends,
You have nowhere,
To see,
Discouraged,
Even from
Seeing your own,
Family!
With the
Elderly,
Living in
Care homes,
Since last
March,
In
Solitary!
Not a good
Situation,
From them
In
To be,
Their children
And
Grandchildren
They are
Not allowed
To see!
Creating
Disharmony,
Amongst
Many!
If you
Get married
Or die,
The people
At your
Wedding
Or
Funeral,

Are
Limited
To Twenty!
What is the
Future,
For
Humanity?
Now they
Want to make,
Vaccinations
Mandatory!
For a
Strain,
Of the flu,
Known as
COVID!
Which we
Hadn't even
Heard about,
One year
Ago,
Funnily!
But in that
Time,
They now
Tell us,
That if
You get
The injections,
That you,
Will be free!
Smells
Fishy
To me!
Especially,
As you
Would still
Have to wear
A mask,
Indefinitely!
This is
A
New
World

Order,
Or
One
World
Government
Moving in,
Surreptitiously
And
Secretly!

Seedy!

Not sure,

If

This,

Has been,

Photoshopped?

It could

Easily be!

But such

A

Sight,

Would

Bring,

Great

Delight,

To some,

Downtown

Bars,

That

Are,

Quite

Seedy!

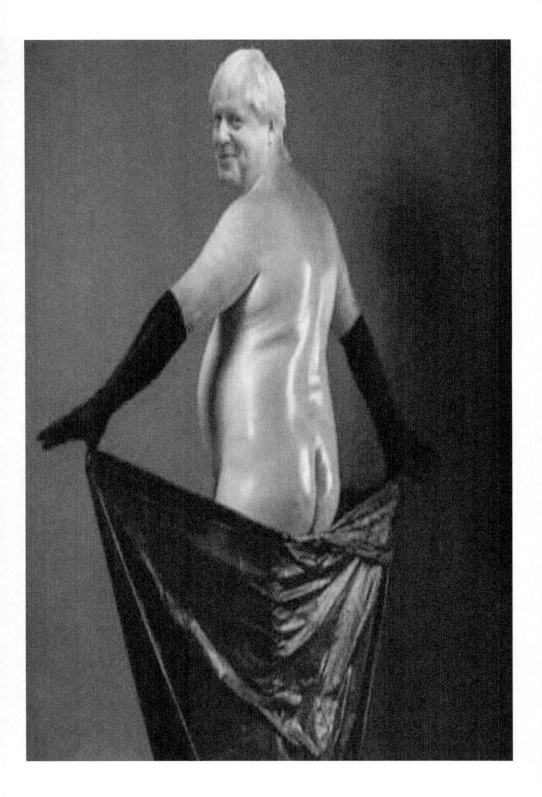

Silently!

The

Snowflakes,

Falling

Slowly,

Like

White

Spiders,

Down

A

Web,

As

Winter

Starts,

In

Scotland,

With

The

Seasons,

Flowing

Ebb!

Peace,

All

Around,

Is to

Be

Found!

No other

Movement

Do you see!

As it

Blankets,

The

Ground,

In

White,

Silently!

Smokes As Well!

Now

Here,

Is

A

Real

Character,

You

Can

Tell!

Aly Widtink,

He

Even,

Has

A

Crow,

That

Smokes,

As

Well!

So true!

A plumber came round

To the house of my mate!

"Do you have any ID?"

He was asked,

"No I dont!"

This my friend,

It did

Frustrate!

"Well,

Let me see

Your face!"

After removing

His mask,

What he saw,

Was a

Disgrace!

His face

Was full of scabs,

Looked like Herpes

Around the lips too!

"The inside of it

Was filthy,

Like a

Witches brew!"

"I have cleaner

Used underpants,

Than the inside

Of his mask!"

He told me

So true!

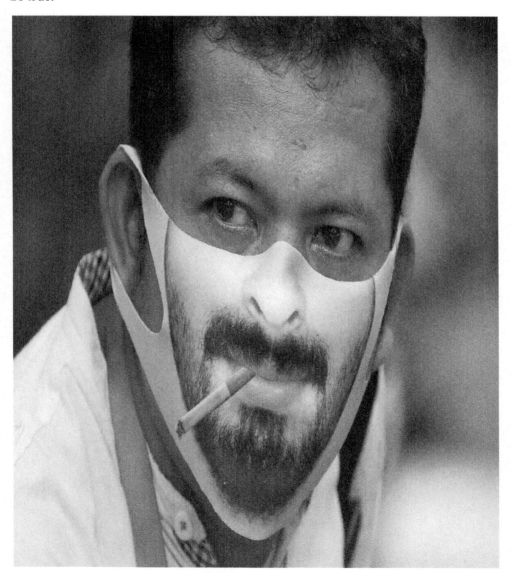

Spray!

This photo

Was taken

On the

19th of

January,

2020!

With a

Strange

Cloud

Formation

Above it,

As you

Can see!

Will

The

International

Cloud

Atlas

Include it

In

Their

Selection

Of

New type

Clouds

Which

Now

Occur

So,

Frequently!

I really

Dont know,

What

To say?

Should we

Call it,

"Some

Stitches,

By

Spray?"

State Capture Gives Me The Blues

Talk of State Capture
In the government!
Billions of Rands
Stolen or misspent!
Talk of State Capture
In the government!

Minister of Finance!
You want the job?
Do what we tell you
Then we can rob!
Talk of State Capture
In the government!

Law unto themselves
Do what they will!
Bribery and corruption
Will make us ill!
Talk of State Capture
In the government!

Thuli's report when will we see?
Sure to create disharmony!
Talk of State Capture
In the government!

Media covers do we see
With own newspaper and TV!
Talk of State Capture
In the government!

The Floor!

The Flaming Lips

Held a live concert

And did not

Want from the

Authorities,

Any trouble,

So they had

One hundred

Inflatable balloons

Made,

So that each

Audience member

Was inside,

Their

Own bubble!

Even the band

Each inside their

Own

Clear

Hemisphere!

Blasting out

Their sounds

For the ones

Who

Hold them near!

Inside each Orb,

Was a

High frequency

Supplemental speaker!

As well as a

Water bottle!

And towel,

In case

Your skin

Should start

To leak in there!

The best bit,

Which is a

Great design,

Was a sign!

"I gotta

Go Pee!"

It says

In good cheer!

With

On the

Other side

"Its Hot

In here!"

If it gets

Too hot!

You can

Get cooled down,

By a portable

Leaf blower,

Which will make

The temperature,

Inside your bubble,

A wee bit lower!

But it could

Be a problem,

When the band

Were playing loud!

And you needed

A pee

But were in

The middle,

Of the crowd!

If it was

Really urgent

And you could

Not wait anymore!

You could always

Pee with abandon,

And know,

That it

Wouldnt,

Stain

The Floor!

The I Am Mantra!

I am

Healthy,

I am

Wealthy,

I am

The

Master

Of

My

Own

Destiny!

I am

Creative,

I am

Prosperous,

I am

Generous,

I am

Happy too!

I am

Loving,

Loveable

And

Loved,

Just the

Same

As you!

I am

Poetic,

I am

Positive,

In

Rhythmic,

Verse,

I am

Open

And

Receptive,

To

The

Abundance

Of

The

Universe!

The Smokecreen!

The

Deceit

Being

Forced,

On the

Worlds

Population

Today!

Is absolute

Insanity!

To say

Otherwise,

Would be,

A

Miscarraige

Of

Justice,

To put it,

Another way!

Forcing people

To wear masks,

Decreasing,

The amount

Of

Oxygen,

Reaching

Your lungs,

Will,

On

Earth,

Shorten,

Your

Stay!

But,

"The

World

Is

Overpopulated!"

They,

The

Powers

That be,

Say!

So now,

A

Manfufactured,

Patented

Virus,

Has been

Released,

To

Global

Dismay!

All over

The planet,

New

Rules

And

Regulations,

Have been

Put,

Into

Force

Today!

Creating

Rebreathing,

Exhaled,

Carbon Dioxide,

From behind

Face masks,

Which restrict,

The in out

Natural flow,

Of your,

Throats,

Airway!

Creating

A

Division,

In

Humanity!

Between,

The

Sceptical,

Non beleivers

And those

That read,

The MSM

And watch

Daily,

TV!

Nowadays

You cannot

Believe

Anything,

That you

Hear,

Or

See?

Instigated

By an

Overhyped,

Flu variant,

Which is

Manipulated,

Statistically,

To keep

FEAR,

In the

Minds

And

Hearts,

Of all

Who see!

To follow,

The official

Narrative,

Unquestioningly!

A mass

Thinning,

Of the

Human

Herd,

Secretly,

And

Surrepticiously!

Helped along,

By the effects

Of

60GHz mm

Microwave

Technology!

Which was

Installed,

Rapidly

And

Globally!

In the

Lock Down

Period,

Since last

March,

Discreetly!

By men in

White vans,

Operating,

Under

Vows,

Of

Secrecy!

And the

Cloak

Of

Darkness,

So as,

Not to

Be seen,

By the

Majority!

Who

Sit at

Home,

Under

Self

Imprisonment

And

House arrest,

Unknowingly!

Scared,

Of the new

Virus,

As anyone

Who dies,

From

Anything!

Gets listed

As

"WITH,

C-V-D!"

Why they

Worry

So much,

I do

Not know?

Because,

Even if you,

Were,

To catch it,

There is a

Ninety nine

Percent,

Recovery rate!

With a rapid

Recovery,

Not slow!

And no

Prescribed

Medicines,

To take

If you get it,

Just sit

At home

For fourteen

Days,

Where the

Time,

Will

Pass slow!

Outside of

Your house,

You are

Not allowed,

To go!

The flu,

Has been

Around

For millions

Of years!

Killing many

With

Comprimised

Immune systems,

Leaving the

Bereaved

Left behind,

In

Tears!

With this latest

Man modified,

Variant,

There is

Also a

Ninety nine

Percent chance,

That you

Will not

Catch it!

"So,

What,

Is the

Problem?"

You might ask,

In good wit!

In truth

It is,

A

Trojan Horse,

To get to

The worlds

Population,

To decimate

Their numbers,

By putting

These new

Laws

Into force!

The likes

Of this,

Before,

Has never

Been seen!

The whole

PLANNEDemic

And

SCAMMEDemic,

Being a

Massive

Smokescreen!

To make

Everyone

So scared,

That they,

Will be

Queing up,

For the

As yet,

Uninvented

And

Untested

Vaccine!

With

Bill (God) Gates,

Funding the

Seven main makers,

To make a

Twenty to one,

Return,

On his

Investments,

In them,

Which is,

Quite,

Obscene!

"Seven

Billion

People

Must

Have it!"

You see him

Saying,

On the

Screen!

Although

Have heard,

That

His three

Children,

Dont get

Vaccinated,

Strange that,

Know

What,

I mean?

Does he

Know,

Something

That we dont?

"They will

Not miss,

The second

Wave!"

He and his

Wife,

Smugly

Declared,

In an

Awful scene!

Whilst

Unkown

To the

Majority,

A

New

World

Order

And

One

World

Government,

Gets

Organised,

Behind,

The

Smokescreen!

The TV!

When a

Hypnotist,

Is working,

He bypasses

The

Left brain,

To talk,

Directly,

To the

Right brain,

Without

Any strain!

The

Left brain,

Is the

Logic

Filter,

Which all

Information,

Passes through!

Then the

Right brain,

Accepts

Any

Information,

That it

Receives,

As

Being,

True!

That is

Why,

The

Hypnotist

Can do,

What he,

Does do!

To get

People,

To behave

In

Irrational ways,

Without

Realising

What they do!

Watching the

TV,

Has the same

Effect

On you!

As it bypasses,

The

Left brain

And to

The right,

Goes

Straight

Through!

This,

You will now,

Clearly see!

As you think

That something

Is true!

Thinking,

That they,

Would not lie

To?

Or

Deceive

You?

Tending to

Beleive,

Everything

That

You

See!

Because,

You

Saw it,

On

The,

TV!

Theorists in Conspiracy!

Was a great experience,

So glad that they

Marched all the way,

To the

Glasgow Green,

From

George Square

And back

As a sign

Of

Lock Down

Protest

Solidarity!

They

Made

History!

They

Were

Warned

Beforehand,

Not to

Do it ,

But it

Looks like

The people

From Anti

Corruption

Scotland

And

Save

Our

Children

When in

Numbers,

Are

Free!

Although

Heavily

Policed,

As

We

Could see!

They

Were

Of

Strong,

Scottish

Ancestry!

From

The

Land,

Known

As

The

Land

Of

The

Brave

And

Free!

Who oppose

Tyranny!

Where now,

Is

Democracy?

Only increasing

The rules,

Regulations,

Statutes

And laws

Extremely

Frequently!

With

So many

Changes,

So often,

That it leaves

You

Confused

You see!

Where are

We now?

What are

The new rules?

From

When

To

When?

And

Everyone

Follows

Along,

Blindly!

Getting th e

Daily instructions

For the

Programming TV!

A Daily

Dose of

Fear and statistics,

Constantly!

But

Luckily,

They have

Come up with

A vaccinne

For us all,

Extremely,

Quickly

For a

Strain,

Of

The

Flu,

Known

As

C-V-D!

That

One

Year ago,

We did

Not

Even know about!

Is

Something not,

A wee bit

Smelly?

But,

If you

Are a TV

Watcher ,

It

Brain washes

You easily!

And

Focus your

Attention

On Fear,

Leaving you

Uneasy!

One year ago,

From today,

The 20th

December

2020!

At that time,

We were still

Free!

Do you remember

How great,

That it

Used to be!

Coming up

To Christmas,

Getting together,

With friends

And

Family!

Going out

To bars and

Restaraunts,

With

Live bands,

Music,

Dancing ,

Singing

Or

Bagpipe

Playing?

Constant,

Chatting!

Everyone

Was

Happy!

Is

It,

Now!

Due

To the

Latest

Concocted,

Preplanned,

Orchestrated,

Operation,

Via

The

Mainstream

Media,

We

Are

At

Their,

Mercy!

As

They

Can

Focus

And

Programme

The

Minds,

Of

All

Who

Watch,

Quite easily!

That is why,

At

Lock Down

Protest

Meetings

A

Regular,

TV watcher,

You will

Rarely see!

They would be

Calling us,

C-V-D

Deniers

And

Coronavirus

Sceptics,

On there,

You see!

As

Well

As

Theorists,

In

Conspiracy!

This is True!

There are
Many people,
With the
Latest
Propaganda
And
Constant,
Fear,
In their head!
They worry,
About catching,
The latest virus,
Even when
Lying
In bed!
Because
Every
Single day,
On the news
And in
The newspapers,
To keep
Your mind
Focused
That way!
While at the
Same time,
They are
Taking,
Your
Freedoms
And
Liberties
Away!
Compare this,
To last
February,
Then,
Compare that,
To now!

And
Hopefully,
You
Will see?
That
YOU!
Are
No
Longer
Free!
And
It was
All done,
In the
Name,
Of
OUR!
Health
And
Safety!
Draconian laws,
Were enacted,
Almost
Immediately!
To fine
You,
If need be?
For breaking,
Any of these
Invisible chains,
That tie down,
Our
Misery!
Snitching
On your
Neighbour,
Being
Promoted,
By those,
In
Authority!
To even
Pay the
Informers,

Setting the
Future,
Can you see?
With a home
Invasion,
Being carried out,
In
Aberdeen,
Supposedly,
Lawfully!
Heavy handed,
In their,
Own home,
Uncooperatively!
With a young
Daughter,
Just back from
Hospital,
Suffering
From
Epilepsy!
Some
Neighbour,
Must have
Heard them,
Coming home
And
Phoned the
Hotline,
Immediately!
Then a knock
On the door!
"Get out of
My home!"
The lady
Did roar!
Two men
In uniform,
Forced their
Way into
The house!
A video
Being taken
By the

Young patient,
Worried
And
Crying!
Voices
Shouting,
Bad,
Vibrations
Not good!
On her
Back,
She went
Flying!
Bare feet
In the air!
As upwards,
Her
Phone camera
Did stare!
Capturing the
Flashing yellow,
Rushed
Movements,
And
"She
Has,
Epilepsy!"
Her
Astounded
Mother,
Crying out,
In
Despair!
Things,
Did not
Turn
Out well,
For the
Family,
That night!
They were
In their
Own home!
And now,

Three
Of them,
Have
Been
Charged,
With
Assault!
Surely
That,
Cannot,
Be right?
Imposed,
Crazy rules,
With little,
That you,
Have to do!
Next time,
The knock,
On the door,
Might be,
For you?
Could end
Up living,
Like
Prince Andrew!
Living quietly
Now,
The
High life,
No more!
And
Getting
A wee bit
Nervous,
Whenever,
There is,
A knock
At
The door!
A wee joke there,
No more!

What are
You not allowed

To do now?
That a
Year ago!
You could do it,
But now you cant,
Because it has
Been closed down,
No longer,
Do the
Bars and restaurants,
Cinemas and theatres,
With happy
Customers flow!
The streets
Are like
Ghost
Towns now!
There is
No where
To go!
Not allowed
To gather,
Or socialise?
Also
No drinking
Coffee
And
Chatting,
As you go!
How bloody
Ridiculous,
How far
Further?
How more
Extreme,
In this
Lock Down,
Can they go?
"Just to
Get the
CASES,
Numbers
Down!"
They,

Will have,
You know!
As your future,
Swills down
The drain,
When?
And
Where?
Can you
Start again?
With now,
No income
Or wage?
For what
Seems,
An
Age!
Millions
On
Furlough
And
Getting
Nervous,
About
The
Next
Stage!
No jobs
Anywhere,
Leaving little,
That you,
Can do!
Than
Sit at home
And watch
The TV,
So that
They,
Can
Keep in touch,
With you!
And
Tell you,
In

Scotland,
Now daily!
Statistics
And
Fear,
Constantly!
Making
Mask wearing,
On all ages,
Mandatory!
To have
Children,
Wearing
Masks
Is
Insanity!
They must
Breathe free!
Growing as
They are,
Daily!
Exhaling
Toxins
And then
Reinhaling
Them,
For anyone,
Is not
Healthy!
As
They
All,
In time,
Will see!
How can
The
Government,
Impose,
An
Unsafe,
Condition,
On the
Majority?
Of

Humanity!
As this
Overhyped,
Inflated,
Preplanned,
Respiratory
Emergency!
Which gave
The
Government
Special powers
In times
Of
Pandemic,
Emergency!
The
Outcome
Of which,
We can
Now see!
We,
Are,
No
Longer,
Free!
Can you
Not see?
Increasing
Authoritarianism
And
Baffling rules,
Which change,
Constantly!
Reminded daily,
The
Political leaders
Followed by some,
Slavishly!
Or
Cultishly?
Maybe,
Make some
Money,
"A call

Tae the
Boys
In
Blue,
An its,
Sum money,
Tae me!"
Mentality!
Divide
And
Rule,
Once more,
Being
Played
Out,
Supremely!
The whole thing
Is being destroyed,
Where now,
Is our,
Economy?
Do you
Really
Beleive,
That after
A vaccine,
That you,
Will be free?
you will,
Still,
Have to wear,
A mask and
Social distance,
Still,
Self isolation,
With no visiting,
Any supportive
Friends,
Or family?
Just another
One injection!
Will then
Be needed,
You will see!

You might
Be a
Mix n Match,
Vaccine
Candidate,
Experimentaly!
With a
Potentialy,
DNA
Modifying
And
Sterilizing,
Cocktail,
Injected,
Quickly!
There
Might be,
Effects?
In one
Form,
Or
Another?
Some of
Them
Severe
And
Permanently!
With no
Come back,
On the
Vaccine
Company!
Now you
Are looking at,
People,
Staring
Over the top,
Of masks,
"Black Sheep!"
Who dare,
To
Breathe free!
People,
Who

Dont,
Watch,
TV!
And
Are not all,
Caught up,
In the
Programming,
Hype,
That makes
A TV watchers,
Reality!
In the UK
That is by far,
The
Majority!
The
All consuming,
Fear,
Of
Dying
From?
Or giving
Someone,
C-V-D?
Such a
Pity!
We have
Had the,
Flu here
Every year,
Since
They built,
The
Callanish
Stones,
But the
People
Always
Persevered,
Sometimes
Chilled,
To the
Bones!

But we,
Are still here,
We used
To be,
In good cheer!
Remember that?
Wasn't 2019,
A good
Year?
When we
Used,
To live
Free!
To do,
Whatever we wanted!
Whenever we wanted!
With
Whoever we wanted!
I would
Love
To do,
That now myself,
Wouldn't you?
A
Question,
Do you,
Really,
Honestly,
Think that,
All of this,
Is because,
Of
The flu?
I feel sorry,
For you,
If you do!
As
Immenent
Changes,
Will be
Happening,
To you!
Bill Gates,
On the

Vaccines,
Will be
Making,
A
Hundred
Billion,
Dollars,
Or two?
Moving
His position,
Up the
Richest man,
In the world
Chart,
From
Number
Three,
To
Number,
Two!
We
Are
In
The
Process,
Of
A
One
World,
Government,
Take over,
Mark my words,
You will see!
Ultimately!
That this,
Is True!

Time!

Watching
The hail,
Falling
In the
Breeze,
Under the
Street light!
Now one o clock
In the morning,
Everyone
In bed now,
Snuggled up,
Warm and
Tight!
When they
Wake up,
In the morning,
The ground,
Will be white!
Looking
Forward,
No doubt,
To a
Stornoway
New Year!
Which is
Always,
An
Occasion,
Filled,
With
Whisky,
Greeting,
Hand shaking,
Hugging,
Slainte va's
Dancing,
Auld
Lang
Syne

And
Good cheer!
Wonder,
How,
It is
Going,
To
Work out,
This year?
As all
The telly
And news,
Has been
Giving us,
Daily,
Is
C-V-D,
FEAR!
Locking
Us
Down,
With
Little
That we,
Can do,
And
All,
They say,
Because
Of
The Flu!
With the
Winter
Temperature,
Here
Sometimes,
It
Chills you,
To your
Bones!
But
We,
Have
Had,

The
Flu here,
Since
The
Coves,
Four
Thousand
Years ago,
Were
Building,
The
Callanish,
Stones!
But life
Went on,
The sick,
Were
Isolated,
Others,
They
Would
Not see!
As
Everyone
Carried on,
Contributing,
To
The
Islands,
Economy!
Nowadays,
We are,
No longer
Free!
Getting
Dictated to
By a
Nationalist
Government,
Who are acting
Under powers,
Of a
Pandemic,
Emergency!

Doing all
These
Things,
In the
Name,
Of
Our,
Health
And
Safety!
But with,
Some dire
Effects,
From
Lock downs,
Seen
Already!
Across
The
Whole
Country!
With
People,
Living
In
Social
Isolation,
In
Care homes,
In
Solitary!
No one
Allowed,
To see,
The
Elderly!
Many
A lonely,
Grandad
And
Granny!
Millions,
Suffering
From

Stress,
Depression
And
Anxiety!
From
Listening,
To the
Daily
Breifings
And
Propaganda,
Being
Shown,
On the
Telly!
Statistically!
But now,
Eyes,
Are
Opening,
As
More
Do see,
The
Insanity!
Of
Draconian
Laws
And
Fines,
Changed,
Almost
Daily!
Boats
Now
Tied up,
At
The
Piers!
With
Imposed,
Restrictions,
Known,
As

Tiers!
Social
And
Family
Bonds,
Being
Ripped
Apart,
Unemployment
Rampant,
Leaving
Many,
In
Tears!
Increasing
Frustration!
In
This,
Once
Proud,
Nation!
I
Tell
You,
This
Story,
In
Rhythm,
Metre
And
Rhyme!
And
Would
Like to,
Let it be
Known,
That
You
Can fool,
Some of
The people,
Some of
The time,
But

You
Cannot,
Fool,
All
Of
The
People,
All
Of
The,
Time!

To Drink!

Heard

Mention,

That

He

Was,

At

The

Time,

The

Rothschilds

Pick!

Quite

Handy,

Under

The

Circumstances,

In

Retrospect

I

Think?

Enough

To

Drive you

To

Drink!

T

oo Big?

Billy Watson:

Nice poems.

I suggest you don't cut off the top of your head in the video frame in future though!

Hi Billy

Having thought

About your

Suggestion!

While on some

Cider

Takin,

A

Swig!

I hope

That its

No

Caused

By,

Ma

Heid,

Bein

Too

Big?

Training History!

I hate the fact that everything is monitored! Every bloody thing that you do! From e
mails to phone calls Facebook and now WhatsApp too! They stopped us from meeting
at Glasgow green last week, two Van's filled with people wearing uniforms in Blue! In
the middle of a park, totally peaceful but they did not want us meeting in more than
groups of two! So they waited until we grudgingly departed, then they did too! What on
earth has the world now come to? We are all being Bullshitted and Lied to! With the
Majority, listening to the ongoing fear and instructions from the TV and MSM through
and Through! As Goebells said, tell a lie enough and it is believed as the truth, we now
see that this is true! In Scotland for Eternity we have had every winter The Flu! We just
carried on, isolated and cared for the sick, they either did, or did not make it through!
We had to carry on doing what we do! But since last March, loud bells of Alarm, with
Draconian new laws enacted totally lacking any charm! Put under Lock Down For
three weeks to flatten the curve, they did say! That was when they started taking our
rights away! We are still under house arrest, not allowed to travel anywhere, millions of
people in Solitary, at blank walls they stare! With the elderly in Care homes, not
allowed to get visits from family! No others are you supposed to see! Minimise exposure
to C _V_D! Does nobody yet realise that we are in fact, no longer free! We are now
under a One World Government and New World Orders planning and
instrumentational strategy! Unfolding and gripping tighter daily! The miracle vaccines
have now arrived, heard say that they, will be mandatory! From seven different makers,
what a cocktail of Chemistry about to go into and out of the majority of Humanity!
Finding its way into nature ultimately, Poisoning it, most definitely! Heard say the
world is overpopulated anyway! People on Government benefits have no choice, they
and their children must be vaccinated or they take the benefit away! Travel Passports
ID2020 on it's way! Our economies destroyed deliberately! Unemployment, suicides,
bankruptcies, domestic abuse, rising greatly! Social circles ripped apart, what was our
Normal life just Twelve months ago, is now History, never more to be! With actions
being taken Globally! With Bill (God) Gates being involved from A to Z! Funding the
patent holder of the virus, event 201, now also the seven main vaccine makers as we can
see! Yet he comes on TV, with flailing hands telling us what must happen in this vital
Pandemic Emergency! Everyone on the Planet must get the shots! He proclaimed
proudly! Apart from many other things, he is also a vaccine salesman, do you not see?
He is a computer nerd who has Zero medical training History!

True!

The TV passes

The left brain,

The logic side!

Which filters

Information,

Before

Going

Through,

To the

Right brain,

Where it

Does reside!

This is

What happens

This is true!

There is little,

That you

Can do!

The right brain,

Accepts

Any

Information,

That comes

Through,

As being

True!

Valley!

This must

Have been,

A sight

To behold,

Seeing

And

Hearing,

Mbongeni

Playing

My

Drum

The Big Yin,

He

Has

Astounding,

Strong,

Pulsating

African

Rhythms

As

He takes

You along!

One thing

That

Without

Hearing,

I do

Forsee!

That day,

They would,

Have been,

Listening

To these,

Rhythms,

In the

Next,

Valley!

Viking Ancestry!

Oh,

Isle of my birth,

You are

Freedom to me,

From the

Stresses

And

Strains,

Of the

Big

City!

With

Your

Moorlands

And

Beaches,

By the

Rolling sea!

The

Heart

Of

The

Homeland,

From

Our

Viking,

Ancestry!

We Can See Through!

Sue Laurel Shaw:

YUP! If people would just RESEARCH this vaccine NoONE would take it. The cognitive dissonance is very strong in this world. FFS THEY SKIPPED ANIMAL TRIALS!! ▶▶▶▶▶▶

You know WHY? Because EVERY single past corona virus vaccine attempt has FAILED!! Yes orginally the animals obtained immunity but when exposed to the virus again, they ALL had massive organ failures and DIED! #2 ITS AN EXPERIMENT, NEVER BEEN USED ON HUMANS BEFORE, #3 Totally DIFFERENT technology, #4 they're IMPLANTING shit into your DNA 🤦

#5 99.9% of people LIVE through the covid FLU FLU FLU!!! I do NOT understand the blind faith!

David Nicoll:

It is really difficult to see what the problem is? As there is a 99% chance that you wont catch it and a 99% recovery rate even if you do! This is truly an overexagerated and hyped up flu! Well planned out and thought through! To ultimately get everyone, to get injections and stand in a queue! Believing everything on the telly, that they tell you too! Luckily, some of us, the Smokescreen, we can see through!